THE ESSENCE OF Z

THE ESSENCE OF COMPUTING SERIES

Published Titles

THE ESSENCE OF Z

Ed Currie
Manchester Metropolitan University

Prentice
Hall

An imprint of Pearson Education

Harlow, England · London · New York · Reading, Massachusetts · San Francisco
Toronto · Don Mills, Ontario · Sydney · Tokyo · Singapore · Hong Kong · Seoul
Taipei · Cape Town · Madrid · Mexico City · Amsterdam · Munich · Paris · Milan

Pearson Education Limited
Edinburgh Gate
Harlow
Essex CM20 2JE
England

and Associated Companies throughout the world

Visit us on the World Wide Web at:
http://www.pearsoned.co.uk

First published 1999 by
Prentice Hall Europe

© Prentice Hall Europe 1999

Typeset in 10/12pt Times
by Aarontype Limited, Bristol

Printed and bound by CPI Antony Rowe, Eastbourne

Library of Congress Cataloging-in-Publication Data

British Library Cataloguing in Publication Data

A catalogue record for this book is available from
the British Library

ISBN 0-13-749839-X

Transferred to digital print on demand, 2007

Contents

Preface

The aim of this book is to provide an elementary introduction to the Z language, which emphasises the practical application of the language to the modelling of systems.

The importance of formal specification in general, and Z in particular, has received growing recognition in recent years, and the subject is included in many university computer science and software engineering curricula. However, for many practitioners and students, formal methods is mathematics, and mathematics was the difficult subject at school which they dropped at the earliest opportunity. Some Z textbooks assume a high degree of mathematical sophistication, which reinforces the perception that Z is an inaccessible, peripheral subject, of little use in the 'real' world. This book is accessible to any reader with GCSE level mathematics, and all prerequisite set theory and predicate logic is covered within the book.

For the lecturer, the book is appropriate for supporting a one-semester course, and contains sufficient notes, examples and exercises to enable some degree of open learning to be introduced. This will allow more contact time for working through case studies, or perhaps more advanced material not covered in the book. For the student, the focus on the practical application of the language will make the book more accessible and, dare I say, enjoyable! For the software practitioner who wishes to find out what Z is all about, the book may be used as a 'teach yourself' text, and the case studies included will hopefully encourage further interest.

The book is not intended to be a complete guide to the Z language, nor is it a reference manual. The title *The Essence of Z* implies not just an essential subset of the language, but also the essential skills and practical knowledge required to apply the notation. Each new concept is illustrated with examples and exercises. As you work through the exercises, you will find that you have growing confidence in your ability to use the Z language to write your own specifications. This practical experience will provide a solid foundation for more advanced work, and there are references to more advanced texts for those who wish to undertake further study.

The organisation of the book is as follows. Chapter 1 discusses the rationale for using formal methods in general and the Z language in particular, and provides some context for the material to follow. Z is based on logic and set theory, and Chapters 2 and 3 cover the elements of these subjects which are prerequisite for the rest of the book. Chapter 4 introduces most of the structural elements of Z specifications via the development of a simple example. Chapter 5 describes the process of specification construction, the format of specifications, and presents a complete simple specification. Upon completing this chapter, you should have an appreciation of the 'flavour' of specification using Z. Chapters 6, 7 and 9 build on this material by introducing more sophisticated mathematical structures for constructing more powerful specifications, while Chapters 8 and 10 apply these new structures to the development of two further complete specifications. In Chapter 11, the preceding material is applied in two more complex examples, a timetabling system and a genealogical database. Finally, Chapter 12 briefly points to some more advanced topics with which you may further develop your knowledge of Z.

Acknowledgements

My thanks to Sandra Hartley for her help in preparing the manuscript, Sebastian Danicic for the idea for the timetable example in Chapter 11, the numerous students on the Z courses at the University of North London who were the guinea pigs for much of the material in the book, and to Jackie Harbor of Prentice Hall for her encouragement and patience.

Symbols

$=$	Abbreviation definition
$\circ$	Backward composition
$\leftrightarrow$	Binary relation
$\times$	Cartesian product
;	Composition (relational or schema)
$\wedge$	Conjunction (logical or schema)
'	Decoration for 'after' state variable or schema
?	Decoration for input variable
!	Decoration for output variable
Δ	Delta convention
$\vee$	Disjunction (logical or schema)
dom	Domain
$\lhd\!\!\!-$	Domain anti-restriction
$\lhd$	Domain restriction
$\Leftrightarrow$	Equivalence or schema equivalence
$\exists$	Existential quantifier
$::=$	Free type definition
$\oplus$	Function overriding
id	Identity relation
$\Rightarrow$	Implication or schema implication
$\mathbb{Z}$	Integers
let	Let predicate
$\mapsto$	Maplet
$\mathbb{N}$	Natural numbers
$\mathbb{N}_1$	Natural numbers not including zero
$\neg$	Negation
$\rightarrowtail$	Partial function
$\mathbb{P}$	Powerset
$\subset$	Proper subset
ran	Range
$\rhd\!\!\!-$	Range anti-restriction
$\rhd$	Range restriction
R^*	Reflexive transitive closure
( )	Relational image
$\hat{=}$	Schema definition

\	Schema hiding
pre	Schema precondition operator
$S\,[x\,/\,a]$	Schema renaming
seq	Sequence
$\frown$	Sequence concatenation
$\upharpoonright$	Sequence filtering
iseq	Sequence, injective
seq_1	Sequence, non-empty
#	Set cardinality
\	Set difference
$\cap$	Set intersection
$\in$	Set membership
$\notin$	Set non-membership
$\cup$	Set union
$\subseteq$	Subset
$\rightarrow$	Total function
R^+	Transitive closure
$\forall$	Universal quantifier
Ξ	Xi convention

CHAPTER 1

Why use Z?

Aims

To present a rationale for more widespread use of mathematics in software engineering, and in particular for the use of the Z notation in specifications.

Learning objectives

When you have completed this chapter, you should be able to:

- appreciate the need to apply engineering principles in the development and maintenance of software;
- understand the advantages of using mathematics to model computer systems;
- appreciate the disadvantages of using natural languages to specify precise requirements;
- understand that specification with Z involves creating models of the required system at different levels of abstraction.

1.1 The engineering of software

The need for software developers to adopt engineering principles has been recognised since a NATO conference in 1968, where the term 'software crisis' was used to describe the situation in which software development frequently ran over time and budget, and produced incorrect products. 30 years later, the crisis is still with us. Part of the problem is the use of informal, imprecise methods in specifying what a proposed software system is supposed to do, designing the software and verifying that it meets the original specification.

Electrical, mechanical and civil engineers make use of classical mathematics such as calculus and differential equations in developing their systems and products. Mathematics provides a formal language for modelling systems and reasoning about their properties. It is a common medium by which

1

engineers of different backgrounds, and even different nationalities, can communicate and work together on large projects. Mathematics is used to specify requirements for systems, and to document the properties of completed systems so that those who must maintain or modify the systems have a precise record of what they do. In contrast, the use of mathematics in software development is minimal. Informal, non-mathematical methods are the norm in every stage of the software lifecycle. If we don't use a language which allows us precisely to specify our requirements, then it is hardly surprising that the requirements are often not satisfied.

Another characteristic of the engineering professions is the use of tools, many of which have evolved over long periods of time to be simple, reliable and fit for their intended purpose. This contrasts sharply with many software tools, which are often complicated, unreliable and unfit for their intended purpose!

The longest and most costly part of the software lifecycle is that of maintenance and upgrading, and this is made easier if the properties of the system are clearly and precisely documented. This becomes even more important as more projects involve legacy systems and less involve developing new software from scratch.

A major issue in software development is the reuse of software components. Despite this being a current hot topic, recent surveys have shown that there is very little reuse of software components in the software industry, except at the level of simple abstract data types. For effective reuse, it is important that the developer has documented precisely what the component does.

As with engineering artefacts, software is often developed, maintained and upgraded by teams of people, and it is important to have tools and languages which enable the precise documentation and communication of ideas at all stages in the process. The above factors all support the rationale for the use of mathematics in software development.

1.2 What is a specification?

A specification may be characterised as a statement of requirements for a system, object or process. A formal specification is one in which the language of mathematics is used to construct such a statement.

Specifications may be constructed at different levels of *abstraction*. A high level of abstraction means that the specification concentrates on the essentials and ignores the details of the problem, and a lower level of abstraction means the specification includes more details. The process of specification of a complex computer system usually involves considering the problem firstly at a high level of abstraction, and then filling in the details at successively lower levels, until the specification can be expressed as a solution in a programming language. In other words, we may view every stage in the development of a software system as a kind of specification; even the final software is a specification of instructions for the computer. The advent of the object-oriented development paradigm has encouraged a view of the development process as an iterative refinement of a single model, and this is not very far removed from the Z development philosophy. Indeed, there are object-oriented variations of Z (Stepney *et al.* 1992), but discussion of these is beyond the scope of this book.

1.3 Formal versus informal specifications

It is important in writing a specification to be able to make precise, unambiguous statements about the problem. Natural languages have enormous expressive power, and words and phrases have different meanings depending on their context. This power facilitates the creation of great works of poetry and literature, but this very power is a problem when one wishes to make simple, precise statements in specifying a solution to a problem. For example, the statement 'Disabled Toilet' could be read as 'this toilet is out of order'. The latter, in colloquial use, could be taken to mean that the toilet has transgressed in some way! The statement 'The output should be 42' could be interpreted as a requirement or as an observation. Such nuances can, and do, lead to misunderstandings when specifications are written in natural languages.

In the language of mathematics, each statement has only one meaning, irrespective of context, and mathematical specifications are therefore precise and unambiguous. Mathematics also enables us to reason about our specification. For example, we can identify properties that the system should have and verify these properties by formal proof. Errors discovered at this stage are relatively cheap to fix, as little abortive work has been done. This may be contrasted with the use of informal techniques, where such discrepancies are more likely to emerge during the later stages of design or when the final program is tested, incurring much greater costs.

In practice, a formal specification will usually be a combination of mathematical notation and English descriptions. The English explanations complement the mathematical notation, and describe aspects of the problem not amenable to description using mathematics. There will often be more English than mathematics in a typical specification document. In addition to the English descriptions, diagrams and pictures may be used, and indeed formal specifications can be employed in conjunction with structured methods such as SSADM.

It is probable that the use of formal methods in the software industry will continue to increase, motivated by factors such as the increasing use of litigation against software developers when systems go horribly wrong, the increasing number of projects successfully completed using formal methods, and increasing awareness by clients of the benefits. For example the UK

Ministry of Defence draft standard for software in safety-critical systems (MoD 1989) requires the use of formal methods.

1.4 The Z language

Z provides a simple, precise, mathematical language for description and communication, and various tools are available to support its use.

Z is a formal specification language based on set theory and logic. It is probably the most popular formal specification language currently available. Z was created by Jean-Raymond Abrial and developed by the Programming Research Group at Oxford University. The accepted reference for the language is Spivey (1992), and ISO/BSI standards for the language are currently under development. Z has been used successfully in some well-documented real industrial systems, and is widely taught in universities.

To write a specification in Z, discrete mathematical structures are used to create a model of the required system, and predicate logic is used to state precisely the required relationships between the structures, thus defining the set of possible valid states for the system. These mathematical structures are more abstract and problem-oriented than the data structures available in most programming languages, and their use is sometimes referred to as representational abstraction. The next stage is to use logic precisely to define the required effect of operations required in the system. The philosophy is to specify *what* each operation is supposed to do, and not *how* it is to do it. This so-called procedural abstraction may feel strange to those familiar with conventional procedural programming languages in which programs are 'recipes'; that is, lists of instructions which, if followed, achieve a desired result. It will come more naturally to those familiar with, for example, functional programming languages, in which a program is effectively an expression which specifies what is to be calculated, and not how this is to be done.

Often a Z specification is first written at a high level of abstraction, and then gradually refined, adding more details, until the mathematical structures used can be easily translated into programming language data structures, and the operations can be implemented as procedures and functions in the target programming language. Formal (mathematical) proof may be used to gain more confidence in the correctness of a Z specification, and ensure that as we refine abstract specifications into more concrete ones, and ultimately into programming language code, each refinement is consistent with and preserves the desired properties of its predecessor.

This book concentrates on the use of Z for the modelling of systems. The topic of formal proof is beyond the scope of the book, and is only superficially mentioned. However, formal proof is an important advantage of using Z, particularly for the specification of safety-critical systems, where the considerable extra investment in time and money is justified.

1.5 Warning!

Z is not a panacea. A language is only as good as the person using it, and a formal language is not a substitute for careful thought. Creating correct, understandable, easily modified computer software is an extremely difficult and complex task. To do it, one must think long and deeply about the problem. Sometimes, after many hours or days of working on a problem, one may realise that an important detail has been neglected. There is no substitute for this process, and it is well known that the more thinking that is done at the earlier stages in a project, individually as well as with colleagues and clients, the less problems are likely to arise later in the project, when the costs incurred will be much greater. A formal language can, however, accurately document the results of this thinking, can act as a precise medium for communication of ideas, and can enable better verification that the final product does what it was supposed to do. Communication with the client is particularly important. Even when the developers have correctly expressed *their* interpretation of the requirements in Z, it is important to ensure that this is a correct description of the client's view.

CHAPTER 2

Logic

Aims

To introduce those elements of propositional and predicate logic which are prerequisite to the study of the fundamentals of Z.

Learning objectives

When you have completed this chapter, you should be able to:

- appreciate the importance of logic in the field of computing in general and formal specification in particular;
- draw truth tables for simple logic expressions;
- recognise tautologies, contradictions and logically equivalent expressions;
- convert between English sentences and logic expressions containing predicates, and understand the compromises necessary to do so.

2.1 Introduction

We all use logic in our daily lives when we attempt to draw valid conclusions from information we are given; in other words, logic is about reasoning. The mathematics of formal logic was developed by George Boole (1815–1864), in an attempt to describe human thought processes. In 1938, his *boolean algebra* was successfully applied to the design of switching networks by Claude Shannon, and more recently has found wide application in the field of computing, for example in design of computer circuits, control flow in programs, reasoning about properties of programs, and as a description language and reasoning mechanism for formal specification languages such as Z. This chapter, of necessity, contains only those bare essentials of propositional and predicate logic which are required for our study of the essence of Z; for a more comprehensive introduction, the reader is referred to Kelly (1997).

2.2 Propositions

A *proposition* is a statement which is either true or false, but not both. These truth values are represented by T and F respectively. The following are all propositions:

'This book is about Z.'
'There is a z in the word zoo.'
'The Earth orbits the Moon.'
'42 < 42'
'Liverpool are the best football team in England.'
'All cats wear hats.'
true
false

The last two are constant propositions, always true and always false respectively.

Questions and commands are not propositions. For example, the following are not propositions:

'Is the answer 42?'
'Don't talk to me like that!'

Exercises 2.1

1. What are the truth values of the above propositions?
2. Why is $x > 0$ not a proposition?

For brevity, the letters P, Q, R, S, etc., are often used to stand for propositions.

2.3 Compound propositions and logical connectives

The propositions above are *atomic*; that is, they are indivisible truth-valued statements. In everyday situations, we combine such propositions with words such as *and*, *or* and *not* to produce *compound propositions*. For example,

'This book is about Z and all cats wear hats.'
'There is a z in the word zoo or the Earth orbits the Moon, and Liverpool are the best football team in England.'
'There is not a z in the word zoo.'

Note that although such sentences do not always make sense, they are valid propositions; that is, they do have a truth value.

In formal logic, the words *and, or* and *not* are logical connectives, or operators. They are represented by the symbols ∧ (conjunction), ∨ (disjunction) and ¬ (negation) respectively. The symbols ∧ and ∨ are binary operators; that is, they are placed between two propositions to construct a new proposition. The symbol ¬ is a unary operator, placed in front of a proposition to construct a new one.

We must now define precisely what we mean when we use the symbols ∧, ∨ and ¬ in logic expressions. We can do this by writing down the truth values of the relevant expression for each combination of truth values of its operand propositions (say P and Q), in a so-called *truth table*. The truth tables for the above operators are given in Tables 2.1–2.3.

Table 2.1 *Truth table for* ∧

P	Q	$P \wedge Q$
F	F	F
F	T	F
T	F	F
T	T	T

$P \wedge Q$ is true if and only if P and Q are both true.

Table 2.2 *Truth table for* ∨

P	Q	$P \vee Q$
F	F	F
F	T	T
T	F	T
T	T	T

$P \vee Q$ is true when either or both of P and Q are true.

Table 2.3 *Truth table for* ¬

P	$\neg P$
F	T
T	F

$\neg P$ is true when P is false, and vice versa.

Exercise 2.2

The meanings of ∧ and ¬ are fairly intuitive, but that of ∨ is rather different from our common interpretation. If P is the proposition 'This afternoon I will go to play football', and Q is the proposition 'This afternoon I will go to play golf', what can you say about the above definition of the connective ∨ in comparison with the usual meaning of the word *or* in everyday life? Write down a truth table to capture the latter meaning, using the symbol ⊕ for your connective.

Two more connectives, the implication operator ⇒ and the equivalence or biconditional operator ⇔, are given in Tables 2.4 and 2.5 respectively.

Table 2.4 *Truth table for* ⇒

P	Q	$P \Rightarrow Q$
F	F	T
F	T	T
T	F	F
T	T	T

Table 2.5 *Truth table for* ⇔

P	Q	$P \Leftrightarrow Q$
F	F	T
F	T	F
T	F	F
T	T	T

The implication operator is read as 'P implies Q' or 'if P then Q'. For example, 'if it is a nice day then I will walk to work'. However, propositions constructed with this operator do not have to make sense in everyday language. From the table we can see that the proposition 'if pigs can fly then there is a spaceship in my teacup' is true! A reasonable way to interpret the table is that the last two lines capture the 'if P is true then Q is true' part, and the first two lines capture the fact that if P isn't true, the expression says nothing about the value of Q; it may be true or false.

The equivalence or biconditional operator may be read as 'P is equivalent to Q' or 'P if and only if Q'. For example, 'I fail my exam if and only if I score less than 40%'. The phrase 'if and only if' may be shortened to 'iff', and this abbreviation will be used in this book.

The operators $\wedge$, $\vee$ and $\Leftrightarrow$ associate to the left, while $\Rightarrow$ associates to the right. This means that, for example,

$P \Rightarrow Q \Rightarrow R$ is equivalent to $P \Rightarrow (Q \Rightarrow R)$ and
$P \Leftrightarrow Q \Leftrightarrow R$ is equivalent to $(P \Leftrightarrow Q) \Leftrightarrow R$

The order of precedence of the connectives, from highest to lowest, is $\neg$, $\wedge$, $\vee$, $\Rightarrow$ and $\Leftrightarrow$.

In writing down compound propositions, we can take advantage of these properties to reduce the number of brackets needed. For example,

$$(\neg P) \Rightarrow (Q \wedge R)$$

may be written as

$$\neg P \Rightarrow Q \wedge R$$

and

$$(P \Rightarrow (Q \Rightarrow \neg P)) \Leftrightarrow Q$$

may be simplified to

$$P \Rightarrow Q \Rightarrow \neg P \Leftrightarrow Q$$

2.4 Truth tables for compound propositions

To draw the truth table of a compound proposition with more than one operator in it, we can break the proposition down into its constituent subexpressions, work out the truth tables for these, and then combine the result.

Example
Draw the truth table for the expression

$$(\neg P \wedge Q) \Rightarrow \neg(Q \vee R)$$

First, we will note that the number of rows in the truth table for a given expression is always 2^n where n is the number of distinct logic variables in the expression. There are three distinct logic variables in the above expression, P, Q and R respectively, and therefore the table will have eight rows. The easiest way to write down the permutations of the values of P, Q and R is to fill the first four rows in column P with F and the next four with T. In the next column, we put F in the first two rows, T in the next two, and so on, and finally in the third column we alternate each row with F and T.

We must now identify the 'first-level' subexpressions, according to the precedence and association rules above; that is, we express our proposition in the form

$$\neg\langle exp\rangle$$

or the form

$$\langle exp1\rangle \; \langle op\rangle \; \langle exp2\rangle$$

as appropriate, where $\langle exp\rangle$, $\langle exp1\rangle$ and $\langle exp2\rangle$ are the subexpressions and $\langle op\rangle$ is one of the above operators. If the subexpressions are complex, we would break these down similarly, until we have expressions for which we are able to write down a column in our truth table. For the above example, we can see that it has the form

$$\langle exp1\rangle \; \langle op\rangle \; \langle exp2\rangle$$

with

$$\langle exp1\rangle = (\neg P \wedge Q) \quad \langle op\rangle = \Rightarrow \quad \text{and} \quad \langle exp2\rangle = \neg(Q \vee R)$$

We write down columns for these expressions, and finally combine these columns to give the column for the entire expression. The result is shown in Table 2.6.

Table 2.6 *Truth table for* $(\neg P \wedge Q) \Rightarrow \neg(Q \vee R)$

P	Q	R	$(\neg P \wedge Q)$	$\neg(Q \vee R)$	$(\neg P \wedge Q) \Rightarrow \neg(Q \vee R)$
F	F	F	F	T	T
F	F	T	F	F	T
F	T	F	T	F	F
F	T	T	T	F	F
T	F	F	F	T	T
T	F	T	F	F	T
T	T	F	F	F	T
T	T	T	F	F	T

2.5 Tautology and contradiction

It can be seen that the above proposition is true for some rows of the table and false for others. A proposition which is true for all the rows of the table is called a *tautology*, and a proposition which is false for all the rows is called a *contradiction*.

Example
Establish whether the proposition

$$A = (P \land Q) \lor (P \land \neg Q \land R) \Leftrightarrow P \land (Q \lor R)$$

is a tautology, a contradiction or neither.

We draw the truth table for the subexpressions

$$B = (P \land Q) \lor (P \land \neg Q \land R)$$

and

$$C = P \land (Q \lor R)$$

and then combine these using the operator $\Leftrightarrow$ to obtain the column for the entire expression.

Again, you may wish to break the expression down further, creating more columns, to make the problem more tractable. The result is shown in Table 2.7.

From the final column of the table, we can see that the expression is a tautology.

Table 2.7 *Truth table for* $(P \land Q) \lor (P \land \neg Q \land R) \Leftrightarrow P \land (Q \lor R)$

P	Q	R	B	C	A
F	F	F	F	F	T
F	F	T	F	F	T
F	T	F	F	F	T
F	T	T	F	F	T
T	F	F	F	F	T
T	F	T	T	T	T
T	T	F	T	T	T
T	T	T	T	T	T

Exercises 2.3

1. Draw truth tables for the following propositions, and state whether each is a tautology, a contradiction or neither. Which are *logically equivalent*; that is, which have the same truth table?

    (i) $P \vee (Q \wedge R)$
    (ii) $\neg P \vee Q$
    (iii) $(P \Rightarrow Q) \Leftrightarrow (Q \Rightarrow P)$
    (iv) $\neg (P \vee Q)$
    (v) $\neg (P \wedge \neg Q)$
    (vi)   *false* $\vee$ *true*
    (vii)   *false* $\wedge \neg (P \vee Q)$

2. Read the following paragraph and write a logic expression to determine whether or not to cycle to work, with R standing for the proposition 'it is raining', S standing for the proposition 'the car starts', and P standing for the proposition 'a push start is available'.

    I either cycle to work, or I use my car. If it isn't raining, I cycle to work. If it is raining, I use my car, unless the car doesn't start, in which case I have to cycle in the rain, unless I can get a push start from my neighbour.

2.6 Laws of boolean algebra

Propositional logic (and set theory; see Chapter 3) are examples of *boolean algebras*. There are five basic laws, or postulates, of boolean algebra. For propositional logic, the laws are as follows, with P, Q and R standing for any propositions:

Commutative laws:

$P \wedge Q \Leftrightarrow Q \wedge P$
$P \vee Q \Leftrightarrow Q \vee P$

Associative laws:

$(P \wedge Q) \wedge R \Leftrightarrow P \wedge (Q \wedge R)$
$(P \vee Q) \vee R \Leftrightarrow P \vee (Q \vee R)$

Distributive laws:

$P \wedge (Q \vee R) \Leftrightarrow (P \wedge Q) \vee (P \wedge R)$
$P \vee (Q \wedge R) \Leftrightarrow (P \vee Q) \wedge (P \vee R)$

Complement laws:

$P \vee \neg P \Leftrightarrow true$
$P \wedge \neg P \Leftrightarrow false$

Identity laws:

$P \vee false \Leftrightarrow P$
$P \wedge true \Leftrightarrow P$

Note that all laws come in pairs. Given one valid law, we can derive another one, its *dual*, by replacing all instances of $\wedge$ with $\vee$ and vice versa, and similarly with all instances of *false* and *true*.

2.7 Proof of theorems

Other laws, or *theorems*, can be defined, the validity of which may be proved by using the above basic laws and other, previously proven, theorems.

Proving laws by repeated application of previously derived laws is called *deduction*. Alternatively, we can prove laws by using truth tables. We write down the truth tables for each side of the law, and check that they are identical. This is called *perfect induction*. It can be tedious, but is often easier than proof by deduction.

Example
Prove $P \vee P \Leftrightarrow P$.

Proof:

$P \vee P$
$\Leftrightarrow (P \vee P) \wedge true$ identity law
$\Leftrightarrow (P \vee P) \wedge (P \vee \neg P)$ complement law
$\Leftrightarrow P \vee (P \wedge \neg P)$ distributive law
$\Leftrightarrow P \vee false$ complement law
$\Leftrightarrow P$ identity law

Example
Prove $P \vee true \Leftrightarrow true$.

Proof:

$P \vee true$
$\Leftrightarrow P \vee (P \vee \neg P)$ complement law
$\Leftrightarrow (P \vee P) \vee \neg P$ associative law
$\Leftrightarrow P \vee \neg P$ theorem above
$\Leftrightarrow true$ complement law

Example
Prove $P \lor (P \land Q) \Leftrightarrow P$.

Proof:

$$P \lor (P \land Q)$$

$\Leftrightarrow (P \land \textit{true}) \lor (P \land Q)$ identity law
$\Leftrightarrow P \land (\textit{true} \lor Q)$ distributive law
$\Leftrightarrow P \land \textit{true}$ theorem above and commutative law
$\Leftrightarrow P$ identity law

Note that we have used the operator $\Leftrightarrow$ in the above. This is a part of the language of propositional logic, and, strictly, this means that the above are not laws, but propositions. We should really have used the meta symbol $\equiv$, which does not construct a proposition, but denotes *logical equivalence* of its operands. However, we will not require this symbol in the rest of this book.

Exercise 2.4

Prove the dual of each of the above laws, both by perfect induction and by deduction.

2.8 Variables and types

Z is a *typed* language. To introduce a *variable* (i.e. a name which denotes a value) into a specification, we write a *declaration* associating the name with a *type*, which is the set of all the values which may be associated with the name. The set of all whole numbers (integers), denoted by $\mathbb{Z}$, is a type which is built into the language:

$$\mathbb{Z} = \ldots, -3, -2, -1, 0, 1, 2, 3, \ldots$$

The set of all natural numbers

$$\mathbb{N} = 0, 1, 2, 3, \ldots$$

although actually a subset of the type $\mathbb{Z}$ rather than a type itself, may also be used in declaring variables. For example,

$$x : \mathbb{Z}$$

declares a variable x which may stand for any integer, and

$x : \mathbb{N}$

declares a variable x which may stand for any natural number.

$x, y : \mathbb{N}$

declares two such variables. There are also mechanisms for defining additional types. We will say a lot more about sets and types in the next chapter, but this is sufficient for our present purpose, which is to extend the notation introduced so far by introducing the concepts of *predicates* and *quantification*.

2.9 Predicates

A predicate is an expression containing one or more *free variables* which act as place holders for values drawn from specified sets. Substituting values for all the free variables in the expression yields a proposition. For example, given

$x, y : \mathbb{N}$

the expression

$x = y + 3$

is a predicate with two free variables x and y. Replacing x with the value 4 and y with the value 3 yields a proposition with the value F. Replacing x with 5 and y with 2 yields a proposition with the value T. Thus, a predicate may be viewed as a template for constructing propositions by 'plugging in' values.

Exercises 2.5

1. Given $x, y, z : \mathbb{N}$, which of the following expressions are predicates?

    (i) $(x + 2y) - 7$
    (ii) $x + 10 = x$
    (iii) $(2x + y) \wedge z$
    (iv) $((x + y) < 7) \wedge (z = y)$

2. If we substitute the values $x = 3$, $y = 4$ and $z = 5$ in the above predicates, what are the truth values of the resulting propositions?

2.10 Quantifiers

To construct a proposition from a predicate, we must remove all the free variables. We can remove a free variable either by replacing it with a particular value as above, or by *binding* it by *quantification*.

The universal quantifier

Consider the expression

$$\forall x : \mathbb{N} \mid x < 10 \bullet x + 9 > 12$$

Which may be explained as follows:

$\forall$ is the symbol for the universal quantifier, read as 'for all'.

$x : \mathbb{N}$ is the declaration of the variable which is *bound* by the quantifier. A bound variable is not free, and cannot be replaced with particular values. In the above expression, x stands for any value from $\mathbb{N}$.

$\mid$ is read as 'such that'.

$x < 10$ is an optional *constraint*. If we choose to omit it, then we also omit the symbol $\mid$.

$\bullet$ may be read as 'it is true that'.

$x + 9 > 12$ is the predicate being quantified.

Thus the expression may be read as 'For all natural numbers x such that x is less than 10, it is true that $x + 9 > 12$'. The expression contains no free variables, and is a proposition with the value F.

The general form of a proposition constructed using the universal quantifier is

$$\forall \langle \text{name} \rangle : \langle \text{type} \rangle \mid \langle \text{optional constraint} \rangle \bullet \langle \text{predicate} \rangle$$

which is read as 'for all $\langle$name$\rangle$ of type $\langle$type$\rangle$ such that $\langle$optional constraint$\rangle$ is true, $\langle$predicate$\rangle$ is true'.

The existential quantifier

Consider the expression

$$\exists x : \mathbb{N} \mid x < 10 \bullet x + 9 > 12$$

Here:

$\exists$ is the symbol for the existential quantifier, read as 'there exists at least one'.

The other parts of the expression are as before. The expression may be read as 'There exists at least one natural number x such that x is less than 10, for which it is true that $x + 9 > 12$'. The expression contains no free variables, and is a proposition with the value T.

Note that there may be many natural numbers which make the predicate true; if we want to state that there is precisely one such number, we may use the *unique quantifier* $\exists_1$. The expression

$$\exists_1 x : \mathbb{N} \mid x < 10 \bullet x + 9 > 12$$

may be read as 'There exists *precisely one* natural number x such that x is less than 10, for which it is true that $x + 9 > 12$'. Clearly, the value of this expression is F.

The general form of a proposition constructed using the existential quantifier is

$$\exists \langle \text{name} \rangle : \langle \text{type} \rangle \mid \langle \text{optional constraint} \rangle \bullet \langle \text{predicte} \rangle$$

which is read as 'There exists a $\langle$name$\rangle$ of type $\langle$type$\rangle$ for which $\langle$optional constraint$\rangle$ is true, such that $\langle$predicate$\rangle$ is true'.

Exercise 2.6

Which of the following are predicates, and which are propositions? For those which are propositions, what are their truth values?

(i) $\forall x : \mathbb{N} \mid x = 4 \bullet x > 5$
(ii) $\forall x : \mathbb{N} \bullet (x > 42) \vee (x \leqslant 42)$
(iii) $\forall x : \mathbb{N} \bullet (\exists y : \mathbb{N} \bullet y = 2x)$
(iv) $\exists x : \mathbb{N} \bullet 2 = 3$
(v) $\forall x : \mathbb{N} \mid (\exists y : \mathbb{N} \bullet x = 2y) \bullet x \neq 42$
(vi) $\exists_1 x : \mathbb{N} \bullet x = 42$
(vii) $\forall x : \mathbb{N} \bullet x = y$

2.11 A note about proof

Z is a formal language based on logic and set theory. There are proof theories associated with both propositional and predicate logic, which can be used to prove that Z specifications have various desirable properties and thus to gain more confidence in them. Proof is also useful in refining a more abstract specification into a more concrete one, usually closer in nature to the programming language in which the specification is to be implemented. Proof can give us more confidence that such a refinement retains the properties of the original specification. The use of proof in specifications is important to an advanced study of Z, but is beyond the scope of this book. See Diller (1994) and Woodcock and Davies (1996) for further reading on this important topic.

CHAPTER 3

Sets and types

Aims

To introduce some concepts of basic set theory, the Z notation for sets and types, and the idea of modelling systems using discrete mathematical structures.

Learning objectives

When you have completed this chapter, you should be able to:

- declare atomic and set-valued objects in Z;
- use logic to create set expressions;
- use sets and set operations to model the state of simple systems;
- understand the importance of types in Z.

3.1 Definitions

A *set* is a collection of distinct objects called *elements* or *members*. For example, the set of all people, or the set of all teapots. Every expression in a Z specification belongs to a set called its *type*, and whenever we introduce a new variable, we must declare its type. The type $\mathbb{Z}$ is the set of all integers, that is all whole numbers, and is built into the language. $\mathbb{N}$ is the set of all natural numbers and $\mathbb{N}_1$ is the set of all natural numbers not including zero.

$$\mathbb{N} = 0, 1, 2, \ldots$$
$$\mathbb{N}_1 = 1, 2, 3, \ldots$$

We may also introduce our own so-called *basic types* or *given sets*, by giving the singular name of the required type, in capitals, in square brackets, with an accompanying explanation. For example,

[*PERSON*] the set of all people

Note that no indication is given as to how individual members of the set are represented.

Another way of introducing a new type is by enumerating the names of the elements of the type in a *free type definition*. For example,

$$COLOUR ::= red \mid green \mid blue$$
$$FUEL ::= petrol \mid diesel \mid electricity$$

We introduce *variables*, that is names denoting values from the above types, by writing *declarations*. For example,

$$p : PERSON$$
$$crayon : COLOUR$$
$$powerSource : FUEL$$

A collection of declarations such as this is called a *signature*. *p*, *crayon* and *powerSource* are now the names of variables which may be associated with any single member of their respective types. To declare more than one variable of the same type, we can use a shorthand form as follows:

$$p, q, r : PERSON$$
$$myFavourite, yourFavourite : COLOUR$$

We can test the value of a variable by propositions such as

$$crayon = green$$

3.2 Ways of describing sets

We may describe sets informally by stating a property common to objects which are elements of the set, for example

'the set of all whole numbers which are greater than 3 and less than 10'

In Z, we may describe this set *in extension*, that is we enumerate the elements between curly brackets, separated by commas

$$numset = \{4, 5, 6, 7, 8, 9\}$$

The $=$ sign denotes an *abbreviation definition*, which is used to introduce a global constant into a Z specification. The identifier *numset* becomes a name for the constant value $\{4, 5, 6, 7, 8, 9\}$. Note the difference between this and equality (=), which is a means of constructing a predicate from two expressions of the same type.

For sets which are integer subranges such as this, we may use the equivalent notation

$$numset = 4 \mathinner{.\,.} 9$$

Sets may also be described by a *set comprehension*, whereby we introduce a predicate which characterises members of the set. The form of a set comprehension is

{declaration | predicate • expression}

The declaration introduces one or more bound variables, the values of which are then constrained by the predicate. The form of the elements of the set is then given by the expression. For example, the above set may be described by

$$numset = \{n : \mathbb{Z} \mid n \geqslant 4 \wedge n \leqslant 9 \bullet n\}$$

read as '*numset* is a set defined by declaring an integer and constraining its possible values to be greater than or equal to 4 and less than or equal to 9; the elements of numset are precisely these values'.

If there is only one variable in the declaration, and the final expression is that variable, then the latter may be omitted, so the above example may be written

$$numset = \{n : \mathbb{Z} \mid n \geqslant 4 \wedge n \leqslant 9\}$$

The predicate may be omitted if it is always true, for example

$$evenints = \{n : \mathbb{Z} \bullet 2 * n\} \qquad \text{the set of all even integers}$$

The empty set, that is the set with no members, is represented by $\varnothing$ or { }.

Strictly, types in the Z language must be *maximal*, that is they must not be subsets of any other sets in the specification in which they occur, and therefore $\mathbb{N}$ and $\mathbb{N}_1$ are not actually types but subsets of the type $\mathbb{Z}$. If they were not available in the Z language, we could define them as follows:

$$\mathbb{N} = \{n : \mathbb{Z} \mid n \geqslant 0\}$$
$$\mathbb{N}_1 = \{n : \mathbb{Z} \mid n > 1\}$$

Thus, in a declaration such as $x : \mathbb{N}$, the type of x is actually $\mathbb{Z}$, but with the implicit constraint that x can only take non-negative values.

Exercises 3.1

1. Define the following sets in extension:
   (i) $\{x:\mathbb{N}\,|\,x<4\bullet 3*x\}$
   (ii) $\{x,y:\mathbb{N}\,|\,x<6\wedge y<x\bullet x-y\}$
   (iii) $\{x,y:\mathbb{N}_1\,|\,x<5\wedge y<5\bullet x+y\}$
   (iv) $\{x,k:\mathbb{N}\,|\,x=k^2\wedge x\leqslant 10\bullet x\}$

2. Define the following sets as comprehensions:
   (i) $\{1,2,3\}$
   (ii) $\{0,1,4,9,16\}$
   (iii) $\{0,2,6,12\}$

3.3 Set operations

Membership

The set membership operator $\in$ is used to test whether an object is a member of a set. The expression $n\in S$ is read as 'n is a member of set S'. For the expression to be valid, n must be of the same type as the elements of S. The following are all true:

$green\in COLOUR$
$4\in\mathbb{Z}$
$diesel\in FUEL$

Non-membership is tested using $\notin$. The following are all true:

$green\notin\{red,\ blue\}$
$4\notin\{\}$
$6\notin\{x:\mathbb{Z}\,|\,x\geqslant 0\wedge x\leqslant 10\bullet x*2+1\}$

Exercise 3.2

Which of the following expressions are valid, and, for the valid ones, which are true and which are false?

   (i) $4\in\{4\}$
   (ii) $\forall x:\mathbb{Z}\bullet x\in\mathbb{N}_1\Rightarrow x\in\mathbb{N}$
   (iii) $diesel\in\{5,6\}$
   (iv) $2\in\{x:\mathbb{Z}\,|\,x\in\mathbb{N}\wedge x<0\}$

(v) $\{4\} \in \{4, 5\}$

(vi) $\{x : \mathbb{N} \mid x + 3 = 6 \bullet 2 * x\} \in \{\{4, 5\}, \{6\}\}$

(vii) $\{\} \in \{\}$

(viii) $\{1\} \notin \{\{\{1\}\}\}$

___

Cardinality

The number of elements in a set S is called its *cardinality*, denoted by $\#S$. For example,

$$\#\{2, 4, 6\} = 3$$

The cardinality of the empty set is zero:

$$\#\{\} = 0$$

Set equality

Two sets are equal iff they contain exactly the same members. The following expressions are all true:

$$\{1, 2, 3\} = \{2, 3, 1\}$$
$$\{1, 2, 3\} = \{1, 1, 1, 1, 1, 2, 3\}$$
$$\{\} = \{x : \mathbb{Z} \mid x > 2 \wedge x < 2\}$$

Note that repeated elements are not significant, as an element can only be in a set once. Also, the order in which the elements are written is not significant.

Subset

For any given sets S, T the expression

$$S \subseteq T$$

is read as 'S is a subset of T', and is a predicate which is true iff every member of S is a member of T. The following expressions are all true:

$$\{1, 2\} \subseteq \{1, 2, 3\}$$
$$\{\} \subseteq \{1, 2, 3\}$$
$$\{1, 2, 3\} \subseteq \{1, 2, 3\}$$
$$\{\} \subseteq \{diesel\}$$
$$\{\} \subseteq \{\}$$

Note that the empty set is a subset of every set, and every set is a subset of itself. We can test whether a set S is a so-called *proper subset* of a set T, that is

$$S \subseteq T \wedge S \neq T$$

using the predicate

$$S \subset T$$

Exercises 3.3

1. What are the values of the following expressions?

   (i) $\#\{1, 2, 3\}$
   (ii) $\#\{1, 1, 1\}$
   (iii) $\#\{\{1, 2\}, \{\}, \{3\}\}$
   (iv) $\#\{\{\{1\}\}\}$
   (v) $\#\{\}$
   (vi) $\#\{\{\}\}$

2. What are the values of the following expressions?

   (i) $\{x, y : \mathbb{N} \mid x + y = 5 \bullet 2 * x\} = \{0, 2, 4, 6, 8, 10\}$
   (ii) $\{red\} \subset \{red, blue\}$
   (iii) $\{1, 2, 3\} \subset \{3, 1, 2\}$
   (iv) $\{\} \subseteq \{\{\{1\}, \{2\}\}\}$

Powerset

The powerset of a set S, denoted by $\mathbb{P}S$, is the set of all the subsets of S. For example,

$$\mathbb{P}\{1, 2, 3\} = \{\{\}, \{1\}, \{2\}, \{3\}, \{1, 2\}, \{1, 3\}, \{2, 3\}, \{1, 2, 3\}\}$$

If S is a type, then so is $\mathbb{P}S$. Variables of type $\mathbb{P}S$ take values which are *sets*. Note that

$$\#\mathbb{P}S = 2^{\#S}$$

so in the above example we have $\#\mathbb{P}\{1, 2, 3\} = 2^3 = 8$.

For example, the declaration

$$x : \mathbb{Z}$$

states that x is a variable which can represent integers, while the declaration

$$y : \mathbb{P}\mathbb{Z}$$

states that y is a variable which can represent *sets* of integers. Typical values might be $x = 5$ and $y = \{1, 2, 3\}$.

We can introduce a variable of any type T by a declaration involving not T but an expression whose type is $\mathbb{P}T$; that is, whose value is a subset of T. It is always possible in such declarations to infer the type of the variable from that of the expression. For example, given the definition

$$numset = \{4, 5, 6, 7, 8, 9\}$$

the declaration

$$x : numset$$

simultaneously introduces a variable of type $\mathbb{Z}$ and constrains its value to the set *numset*. Similarly the declaration

$$x : \mathbb{N}$$

simultaneously introduces a variable of type $\mathbb{Z}$ and constrains its value to the set $\mathbb{N}$.

The type of an empty set can usually be inferred from the context in which it appears. For example, in the expression $\{\} \in \{\{1\}, \{2,3\}, \{\}\}$ the type of the empty sets is $\mathbb{P}\mathbb{Z}$.

Exercises 3.4

1. Given the declaration $x : \mathbb{P}(\mathbb{P}\mathbb{Z})$, write down a typical value which may be associated with the variable x.
2. What is the type and cardinality of the following sets?

    (i) $\{\{1\}, \{2, 3\}\}$
    (ii) $\{\{\{1\}\}, \{\{2, 3\}\}, \{\}\}$
    (iii) $\{x : \mathbb{P}\mathbb{N} \mid x \in \mathbb{P}\{1, 2, 3\} \wedge x \subseteq \{1, 2\}\}$

Union

The union of two sets S and T, written as

$$S \cup T$$

is the set consisting of all the members from S and T. For the expression to be valid, the sets S and T must be of the same type. For example,

$$\{1, 2, 3\} \cup \{3, 4, 5\} = \{1, 2, 3, 4, 5\}$$

As a further example, if the set of students at a given university is $[STUDENT]$, we may define the following sets:

skiing: $\mathbb{P}\ STUDENT$ the set of all students in the university skiing club
badminton: $\mathbb{P}\ STUDENT$ the set of all students in the university badminton club

Then the set of all students who are in the skiing club, the badminton club, or both, is

skiing $\cup$ *badminton*

Intersection

The intersection of two sets S and T, written as

$$S \cap T$$

is the set consisting of all the members which are in both S and T. Again, for the expression to be valid, the sets S and T must be of the same type. For example,

$$\{1, 2, 3\} \cap \{3, 4, 5\} = \{3\}$$

From the above example, the set of all students who are in both the skiing club *and* the badminton club is

skiing $\cap$ *badminton*

Generalised union and intersection

Generalised union and intersection are special versions of the above operators, which are applied to a set of sets. The *generalised union* of a set of sets S, written as

 S

is the set comprising all elements which are members of at least one of the members of S. For example,

$$\bigcup\{\{1,2\},\ \{2,3,4\},\ \{1,2,4,5\}\} = \{1,2,3,4,5\}$$

The *generalised intersection* of a set of sets S, written as

$$\bigcap S$$

is the set comprising those elements which are members of all the members of S. For example,

$$\bigcap\{\{1,2\},\ \{2,3,4\},\ \{1,2,4,5\}\} = \{2\}$$

As a further example, if the university also has the following clubs

football, drama, yoga : $\mathbb{P}\ STUDENT$

then the set of those students who are members of at least one of the clubs is

$$\bigcup\{skiing,\ badminton,\ football,\ drama,\ yoga\}$$

and the set of those students who are members of all of the clubs is

$$\bigcap\{skiing,\ badminton,\ football,\ drama,\ yoga\}$$

Set difference

The difference of two sets S and T, written as

$$S \backslash T$$

is the set consisting of all the members of S which are not in T. For example,

$$\{1,2,3,4\}\backslash\{1,3,6,8\} = \{2,4\}$$

As a further example, the set of all students who are in the skiing club and not in the badminton club is

skiing\badminton

Exercises 3.5

1. State whether each of the following expressions is valid, and simplify those which are:
    (i) $(\{1,2,3\} \cup \{2,3,4\}) \cap \{5\}$
    (ii) $\{1,2,3\}\backslash 4$
    (iii) $\{1,2,3\}\backslash\{2,1,3\}$
    (iv) $\{1,2,3\} \cap (\{1,2,3\} \cup \{\{1\}, \{2\}, \{3\}\})$

2. What is the value of the expression $4 \in (\{4,5\}\backslash\{4,2\})$?
3. Given the following,

    $skiing = \{tony, fred, alice, sarah, diana, susan, bill, henry, don\}$
    $badminton = \{colin, sarah, fred, carol, don\}$
    $football = \{bill, colin, alice, don, tony\}$
    $drama = \{sarah, don\}$
    $yoga = \{henry, don, carol, alice\}$

simplify the following expressions:

    (i) $(badminton \cap football)\backslash skiing$
    (ii) $\{x : | x \in \mathbb{P} \ skiing \wedge ((x \cap drama) \subseteq badminton)\}$
    (iii) $\bigcup\{skiing, badminton, drama\}$
    (iv) $\bigcap\{skiing, badminton, football, drama, yoga\}$
    (v) $\bigcap \mathbb{P} \ skiing$
    (vi) $\bigcup \mathbb{P} \ skiing$
    (vii) $\mathbb{P}(\bigcap\{skiing, badminton\})$

3.4 Sets and logic

Before leaving our introduction to sets, it is worth repeating that both elementary set theory and propositional logic are examples of *boolean algebras*. By making correspondences between set operators and logic operators, we arrive at the same five basic laws of boolean algebra which were discussed in Chapter 2. This is important, because it means that every proven logic theorem has an equivalent theorem within set theory, and results proved in one system are valid in the other. However, further discussion of this is beyond the scope of this book.

A major claim for formal specification languages is that they enable the construction of precise, unambiguous statements of requirements. In Z, the languages of sets and logic are the basic tools used to make such statements.

However, you will note that the set operators introduced in this chapter have been described in English. We could have given precise definitions using logic. For example, the following is a definition of set union. For a given type T

$$\forall x : T; A, B : \mathbb{P}T \bullet x \in A \cup B \Leftrightarrow x \in A \vee x \in B$$

In other words

$$\forall A, B : \mathbb{P}T \bullet A \cup B = \{x : T \mid x \in A \vee x \in B\}$$

Exercises 3.6

1. Give logic expressions to define formally the meaning of:
   (i)   set intersection;
   (ii) set difference;
   (iii) generalised union.

2. Describe the following situation using the notation covered in this chapter. Assume that you have the type [PERSON], the set of all people.
   (i)   People are either women or men, but not both.
   (ii) A company employs people in three departments: marketing, personnel and production. Each employee is in precisely one of these departments.
   (iii) Each department has a maximum of 10 staff.
   (iv) All the staff in marketing are women.
   (v)   The company employs more men than women.

3. Now assume that each employee in the previous question can be in more than one department. Write down expressions for:
   (i)   The number of women who work in all three departments.
   (ii) The number of men who work in marketing and personnel but not in production.

CHAPTER 4

The structure of a Z specification

Aims

To apply the material of the previous two chapters to the development of Z specifications, to introduce mechanisms for structuring Z specifications, and to illustrate the above with a simple example.

Learning objectives

When you have completed this chapter, you should be able to:

- represent the state of simple systems using sets and logic;
- specify the effect of operations which change or interrogate the state of a system;
- structure your specifications using schemas;
- introduce appropriate exception handling to totalise your operations using the schema calculus;
- determine the conditions necessary for an operation to take place successfully.

4.1 Introduction

In this chapter, we will develop an example to illustrate the 'flavour' of writing specifications with Z. We will introduce most of the notation for structuring Z specifications that will be used for the rest of the book. The specification is for the student badminton club mentioned in Chapter 3, and could be implemented as a computer system or paper records, to keep track of the whereabouts of the club members, add or remove members from the club, etc.

To write a specification in Z, we create a *model* of the required system. The structure, or state, of the system is represented using sets, and the relationships between the elements of the state are expressed using the language of logic. We then use logic to specify operations to change or make queries about the state of the system.

4.2 The system state

Suppose that the student badminton club has the sole use of a hall with a single badminton court. To use the hall, one must be a member of the club. To ensure that everyone gets enough games, there is a limit of 20 people allowed in the hall at any one time. We will construct a model of this system. We begin by identifying the basic types required in our specification; here there is only one:

$[STUDENT]$ the set of all students

We can represent the limit on the number of people allowed in the hall by an *axiomatic description* which is a Z construct for defining a global variable, which is in scope (may be referred to) throughout the specification.

$$maxPlayers : \mathbb{N}$$
$$maxPlayers = 20$$

The top half is a declaration, and the bottom half is an optional predicate specifying a constraint on the values of the variable declared. The constraint chosen here effectively makes *maxPlayers* a global constant.

We are interested in the whereabouts of the members of the badminton club. We can represent this information using two sets of students: *badminton*, the set of all members of the club, and *hall*, the set of all those who are in the hall. The things which must always be true for any values of these sets are:

1.   A person in the hall must be a member of the club.

$hall \subseteq badminton$

2.   The number of people in the hall must not exceed *maxPlayers*.

$\# \, hall \leqslant maxPlayers$

These predicates are called the *state invariants* of the system. If the sets *hall* and *badminton* are to represent a valid state for the system, then the values which they take must be such that they make the state invariant predicates true.

In Z, we combine the declaration of the sets with the predicates constraining their values using a box called a *schema*. The state schema for our system is as follows:

```
┌─────── ClubState ───────
│ badminton : ℙ STUDENT
│ hall : ℙ STUDENT
├──────────────────────────
│ hall ⊆ badminton
│ # hall ≤ maxPlayers
└──────────────────────────
```

The state variables are declared in the top half of the schema box, above the line. *badminton* and *hall* are variables which take values which are sets of students, so their type is the powerset of the type *STUDENT*. The predicates defining the invariant properties of the state are defined in the bottom half. Note that predicates on separate lines are implicitly conjoined to make one predicate; the above could be rewritten as

$$(hall \subseteq badminton) \wedge (\# \ hall \leq maxPlayers)$$

4.3 Operations

The above state schema defines the set of valid states which our system may assume. The system may move from one valid state to another by *operations* which change the values of one or more of the state variables. For this example, we might be interested in operations to add or remove a member to/from the club, or to add or remove a member to/from the hall. Such operations will involve adding or removing elements to/from the two sets which constitute the state variables. However, before we specify any operations, we must learn some new notation.

Inputs and outputs

Operations often require inputs and outputs, and the convention for naming these is that an input identifier is terminated by a ? and an output identifier is terminated by a !.

'Before' and 'after' states

To specify the effect of an operation on the state of the system, we must be able to refer to the state variables both 'before' and 'after' an operation. The convention is that 'before' variables are undecorated, whereas the names of 'after' variables are decorated with primes (dashes). If x is a variable before a given operation, then x' will be the same variable after the operation. For example, the set *badminton* would represent the variable before an operation, and the set *badminton'* would represent the same variable after the operation.

We define the effect of a state-changing operation using:

1. Predicates which state what must be true about the 'before' state of the system and the inputs, if any, in order for the operation to take place. These are known as *preconditions*.

2. Predicates which relate the 'before' state and the inputs, if any, to the 'after' state and the outputs, if any. These are known as *postconditions*, and define the effect of the operation. Note that we specify *what* the result of the operation must be; *how* the operation works is not stated. This is a consideration for those who must implement the specification as a computer program or other system.

Note that the preconditions may be explicitly stated, or they may be implicit, occurring as a consequence of the postconditions and/or the state invariant, in which case we may have to calculate them. See Section 4.13 for more on this.

4.4 Adding a new member

We will now use the above ideas to specify an operation to add a new member to the badminton club. To join the club, a potential member must register with the club secretary, after which the member may go to the hall to play. The potential new member will be an input for the operation, declared as

$$newMember? : STUDENT$$

For this operation, it is important that *newMember?* is not already a member of the club. This leads to the precondition

$$newMember? \notin badminton$$

Note that the state invariant implies that *newMember?* is also not in the hall. The required behaviour for the operation is that *newMember?* be added to the set *badminton* but not to the set *hall*. We can achieve this by placing *newMember?* in a set by itself (a singleton set), and taking the union of this set with the set *badminton*. This leads to the following postconditions:

$$badminton' = badminton \cup \{newMember?\}$$
$$hall' = hall$$

Note that we have explicitly specified that the set *hall* does not change. If we didn't include this condition, we would be underspecifying the operation, that is we would not be stating whether or not *newMember?* is to become an element of *hall*. A person implementing this operation could then make either choice. It is important in general to specify our operations fully; that is, to state what is to happen to all of the state variables.

To complete the definition of the operation in Z, we gather the above declarations and predicates into an *operation schema* which we will call *AddMember*. The declarations part (top half) of the schema must contain the declaration of any input and output variables. As things stand, *AddMember* would also have to contain the 'before' and 'after' versions of the state schema declarations and invariant predicates. This is because all declarations and predicates are local to the schema in which they appear, and are therefore not implicitly available in any other schema. Any object referred to in the predicate part (bottom half) of a schema must either be declared in the top half of that schema or be globally defined.

We could simply copy all the required 'before' and 'after' state declarations and predicates into our *AddMember* schema, as follows:

$$
\begin{array}{|l}
\hline
\quad\quad\quad AddMember \\
\hline
badminton : \mathbb{P}\ STUDENT \\
badminton' : \mathbb{P}\ STUDENT \\
hall : \mathbb{P}\ STUDENT \\
hall' : \mathbb{P}\ STUDENT \\
newMember? : STUDENT \\
\hline
hall \subseteq badminton \\
\#\ hall \leqslant maxPlayers \\
hall' \subseteq badminton' \\
\#\ hall' \leqslant maxPlayers \\
\\
newMember? \notin badminton \\
badminton' = badminton \cup \{newMember?\} \\
hall' = hall \\
\hline
\end{array}
$$

However, this could get very tedious, and Z provides the following mechanisms for simplifying the process, thereby making specifications clearer and more succinct.

Schema decoration

Given a schema S, the notation S' stands for S with all of its variables decorated with primes throughout the schema. For example,

$$
\begin{array}{|l}
\hline
\quad\quad\quad ClubState' \\
\hline
badminton' : \mathbb{P}\ STUDENT \\
hall' : \mathbb{P}\ STUDENT \\
\hline
hall' \subseteq badminton' \\
\#\ hall' \leqslant maxPlayers \\
\hline
\end{array}
$$

The required schema is

```
┌─── EnterHall ──────
│ Δ ClubState
│ enterer? : STUDENT
├────────────────────
│ enterer? ∈ badminton
│ enterer? ∉ hall
│ # hall < maxPlayers
│ hall' = hall ∪ {enterer?}
│ badminton' = badminton
└────────────────────
```

Exercise 4.2

Write a schema for the operation *LeaveHall*, which removes a member from the hall.

4.6 The xi convention

For a given state schema S, the notation ΞS represents the schema obtained by including ΔS in an otherwise empty schema together with, for every variable x declared in S, the predicate

$$x = x'$$

In other words, including ΞS in an operation schema makes visible the 'before' and 'after' versions of the declarations and predicates of S, together with the assertion that these variables are not changed by the operation. Again, the Ξ symbol is simply part of a schema name, but the convention is universally used.

For the badminton club example, we have

```
┌─── Ξ ClubState ──────
│ Δ ClubState
├──────────────────────
│ badminton' = badminton
│ hall' = hall
└──────────────────────
```

4.7 Query operations

Sometimes we wish to specify operations which do not change the state, but output some information about it. For example an operation to output the set of all club members not in the hall:

```
┌─── NotInHall ───────────
│ Ξ ClubState
│ outside! : ℙ STUDENT
├───────────────────────
│ outside! = badminton \ hall
└───────────────────────
```

Note that the inclusion of Ξ *ClubState* specifies that the operation does not change the state, and the suffix ! in the variable name *outside!* indicates that this is an output. There is no precondition; this operation may be applied to any state.

Exercise 4.3

Specify an operation which inputs a student and outputs a message stating whether s/he is:

(i)   in the hall;
(ii)   a member but not in the hall;
(iii) not a member.

You may assume the existence of the free type

$$MESSAGE ::= inHall \mid notInHall \mid notMember$$

4.8 Combining schemas with propositional operators

Two schemas S and T can be combined using any of the following propositional operators:

$S \wedge T$
$S \vee T$
$S \Rightarrow T$ or
$S \Leftrightarrow T$

Each of these defines a schema which merges the declarations from S and T, and whose predicate is

$$P_s \ op \ P_t$$

where P_s is the predicate of S, *op* is the appropriate propositional operator, and P_t is the predicate of T.

Any variable name occurring in both S and T must have the same type in each.

For example, consider the following schemas:

```
┌─ A ──────        ┌─ B ────────      ┌─ C ────────
│ a : Z            │ a, b : Z         │ b : P Z
├──────────        ├────────────      ├────────────
│ a = 42           │ a = b + 2        │ 42 ∈ b
└──────────        │ b < 10           └────────────
                   └────────────
```

$AandB \mathrel{\widehat{=}} A \wedge B$ is the schema

```
┌──────────── AandB ────────────
│ a, b : Z
├───────────────────────────────
│ (a = 42) ∧ ((a = b + 2) ∧ (b < 10))
└───────────────────────────────
```

$\mathrel{\widehat{=}}$ is the *schema definition symbol*, which is used to associate a name with a schema.

$AimpliesC \mathrel{\widehat{=}} A \Rightarrow C$ is the schema

```
┌──── AimpliesC ────
│ a : Z
│ b : P Z
├───────────────────
│ (a = 42) ⇒ (42 ∈ b)
└───────────────────
```

The use of propositional operators with schemas enables us to give more structure to complex specifications by breaking them down into simpler units. For example, the *AddMember* schema requires that the new member joins the club whilst outside the hall, and the only people allowed in the hall are members of the badminton club. Let us picture a different scenario, where the hall has other activities going on, and people other than members of the badminton club may be present in the hall. The set *hall* is still the set of all members of the badminton club who are in the hall, but it is possible for a new member to join either outside or inside the hall. We can represent the joining location as a free type, and define two operation schemas, *AddMemberInHall* and *AddMemberOutHall*, to specify the two possible cases as follows:

$LOCATION ::= inside \mid outside$

```
┌──── AddMemberInHall ──────────────
│ Δ ClubState
│ newMember? : STUDENT
│ where? : LOCATION
├──────────────────────────────────
│ where? = inside
│ newMember? ∉ badminton
│ # hall < maxPlayers
│ badminton' = badminton ∪ {newMember?}
│ hall' = hall ∪ {newMember?}
│
└──────────────────────────────────
```

```
┌──── AddMemberOutHall ─────────────
│ Δ ClubState
│ newMember? : STUDENT
│ where? : LOCATION
├──────────────────────────────────
│ where? = outside
│ newMember? ∉ badminton
│ badminton' = badminton ∪ {newMember?}
│ hall' = hall
│
└──────────────────────────────────
```

We can now define a schema which represents the operation of adding a new member either outside or inside the hall using schema disjunction as follows:

$$AddMemberAnywhere \mathrel{\hat{=}} AddMemberInHall \lor AddMemberOutHall$$

Where an operation schema has explicit preconditions, we can specify separate schemas for handling the exception situations where the preconditions of the operation are not satisfied, and use the schema calculus to combine these schemas to define a robust, so-called *total* version of the operation which does something meaningful for any combination of the values of its 'before' state and inputs. An example of this is presented in the next section.

Exercise 4.4

1. Given the above definitions of A, B and C, write down the expansion of the following schema expressions:
    (i) $P \mathrel{\hat{=}} A \Leftrightarrow B$
    (ii) $Q \mathrel{\hat{=}} A \Rightarrow (A \lor C)$
    (iii) $R \mathrel{\hat{=}} A \lor (B \land C)$

2. What do you notice about the predicate of the schema $A \wedge B$?
3. Give a definition of Δ *ClubState* using a propositional schema operator.

4.9 Totalising operations

When specifying an operation, it is important to state the action to be taken for all possible values of the state variables and inputs. Such an operation is sometimes referred to as *total*. If the operation specification is not total, then the specification is not complete; we are leaving it up to the implementor of the system to decide what to do in the cases not specified.

In the *AddMember* operation, for example, we have only specified what is to happen if the precondition

$$newMember? \notin badminton$$

is satisfied. If the precondition is not satisfied, the successful case of the operation must not happen, the state must not change, and we will want the system to produce an appropriate exception message stating the reason for not doing the operation. A common way of dealing with this in Z is to represent the set of 'outcome' messages as a free type.

$$MESSAGE ::= success \mid isMember$$

We can now write a schema to specify the action for each possible outcome. The situation where a potential new member is *already* a member gives the following schema. Note the inclusion of Ξ *ClubState* to indicate that this schema does not change the state.

```
┌─── IsMember ────────
│ Ξ ClubState
│ newMember?: STUDENT
│ outcome! : MESSAGE
├─────────────────────
│ newMember?∈ badminton
│ outcome! = isMember
└─────────────────────
```

For consistency, we may also wish to produce a message when the operation executes successfully. This message can be represented by the schema

```
 __ SuccessMessage ____
| outcome! : MESSAGE
|_____
| outcome! = success
|_____
```

Schemas may also be written in an equivalent *horizontal form*, where declarations and predicates are enclosed in square brackets and separated by |. If there is more than one declaration or predicate, they are separated by semicolons. The horizontal form is appropriate for small schemas such as *SuccessMessage*:

$$SuccessMessage \cong [outcome! : MESSAGE \mid outcome! = success]$$

The complete specification of the *AddMember* operation can now be defined by combining the various schemas using the propositional operators of the schema calculus encountered above.

$$TotalAddMember \cong (AddMember \land SuccessMessage) \lor IsMember$$

This is a schema which specifies the outcome for any possible values of the 'before' state and inputs, and outputs the appropriate message. Note that some operations have no preconditions and therefore such exception handling is unnecessary. For example, the *NotInHall* operation in Section 4.7 above may be applied to any state and is therefore already a total operation.

For operations with more than one precondition, the neatest way of defining the total operation is to write separate schemas to handle each of the precondition exceptions, and then combine the schemas using schema disjunction as above. However, if more than one error occurs simultaneously, the operation may be non-deterministic in that it does not specify which of the errors are to be reported. This could be overcome by including error messages not just for every individual error condition, but also for all combinations of error conditions. However, this would become extremely tedious and lead to unnecessarily large specifications. A better solution is to document the non-determinism in the specification document, leaving it up to the implementor of the specification to decide how to handle multiple error conditions.

The use of the delta and xi conventions, and the notation for combining schemas using propositional operators, allow us to produce modular specifications which are clearer and more succinct. To demonstrate this, you might try expanding the *TotalAddMember* operation as a single schema!

Exercise 4.5

Extend the specification to totalise the *EnterHall* operation. Note that in this case there are three preconditions to consider, the exception to each of which should be handled by a separate schema.

4.10 The initial state

We have created a model of a system by defining a set of valid states and a set of valid operations, some of which cause the system to move from one state to another. However, we have not specified in which valid state the system must start. An appropriate initial state for this system would be one in which there are no members in the club; that is, in which the sets *badminton* and *hall* are empty.

$$
\begin{array}{|l}
\hline
\_\_InitClubState\_\_\_\_\\
ClubState'\\
\hline
badminton' = \{\}\\
hall' = \{\}\\
\hline
\end{array}
$$

Note the inclusion of *ClubState'*; the convention is for initial state variables to be decorated. The initial state is effectively a special 'after' state, without a corresponding 'before' state. We may think of it as the result of an operation to create our system from nothing, or to reset the system from any state.

We are obliged to verify that the proposed initial state is indeed a valid state; that is, the state invariant property is not violated. A brief inspection in this case confirms that this is so, because

$$\{\} \subseteq \{\}$$

and

$$\forall n : \mathbb{N} \bullet \#\{\} \leqslant n$$

However, for some specifications, the proof that the proposed initial state is valid is not so straightforward.

4.11 Renaming

Schema variables may be renamed to produce a new schema, by writing the necessary changes in square brackets after the schema name. In general, for a schema S, the expression

$$S[x/a, y/b, z/c]$$

represents S with all instances of the name a replaced by x, b by y and c by z.

For example, given the badminton club state schema as before

```
┌─────── ClubState ────────
│ badminton : ℙ STUDENT
│ hall : ℙ STUDENT
├──────────────────────────
│ hall ⊆ badminton
│ # hall ⩽ maxPlayers
└──────────────────────────
```

the schema

$FootyClub \cong ClubState\ [\,football\,/\,badminton,\ pitch\,/\,hall\,]$

is the schema

```
┌─────── FootyClub ───────
│ football : ℙ STUDENT
│ pitch : ℙ STUDENT
├─────────────────────────
│ pitch ⊆ football
│ # pitch ⩽ maxPlayers
└─────────────────────────
```

4.12 Hiding

The schema hiding operator \ takes a schema and a list of variables declared in the schema, and hides the variables in the schema by removing them from the schema declarations and existentially quantifying them in the schema predicates. In general, for a schema S, the expression

$S \setminus (x, y, z)$

represents S with the declarations of variables x, y and z removed and existentially quantified.

Given the schemas A and B from Section 4.8,

```
┌─ A ──       ┌─ B ────
│ a : ℤ       │ a, b : ℤ
├──────       ├────────
│ a = 42      │ a = b + 2
└──────       │ b < 10
              └────────
```

the schema $A \setminus (a)$ would be a schema with an empty signature and a predicate which is always true!

The schema $HideB \cong B \setminus (b)$ would be as follows:

```
┌─ HideB ──────
│ a : ℤ
├──────────────
│ ∃ b : ℤ •
│   a = b + 2
│   ∧ b < 10
└──────────────
```

In fact, the predicate now simply states that there is a number less than 12 which equals a, so the schema simplifies to

```
┌─ HideB ─
│ a : ℤ
├─────────
│ a < 12
└─────────
```

Given the *AddMember* schema as before,

```
┌───── AddMember ──────────────────
│ Δ ClubState
│ newMember? : STUDENT
├───────────────────────────────────
│ newMember? ∉ badminton
│ badminton' = badminton ∪ {newMember?}
│ hall' = hall
└───────────────────────────────────
```

the definition

$AddWho \cong AddMember \setminus (newMember?)$

is the schema

```
┌───── AddWho ──────────────────
│ Δ ClubState
├────────────────────────────────
│ ∃ newMember? : STUDENT •
│   newMember? ∉ badminton
│   ∧ badminton' = badminton ∪ {newMember?}
│   ∧ hall' = hall
└────────────────────────────────
```

Hiding may also be achieved using *projection*. See Spivey (1992) for further information.

4.13 Operation schema preconditions

When we specify an operation, it is important to know the combinations of the 'before' state and input variables for which the operation may be applied. In other words, the combinations of 'before' state and input variables for which there are values of the 'after' state and output variables which satisfy the operation's predicates. These combinations may be defined from the operation schema by hiding all 'after' state variable and outputs.

The schema precondition operator, denoted by pre, is used to calculate the precondition of an operation schema. For an operation schema S, the expression

pre S

is the precondition schema of S, which is S with all 'after' state variables and output variables hidden. For example, consider the schema *SuccessAddMember* specifying the successful addition of a member:

$SuccessAddMember \cong AddMember \wedge SuccessMessage$

If we expand this schema, making all 'after' state declarations and predicates explicit, we get the following:

```
┌─── SuccessAddMember ───────────
│ ClubState
│ badminton' : ℙ STUDENT
│ hall' : ℙ STUDENT
│ newMember? : STUDENT
│ outcome! : MESSAGE
├────────────────────────────────
│ hall ' ⊆ badminton'
│ # hall ' ⩽ maxPlayers
│
│ newMember? ∉ badminton
│ badminton' = badminton ∪ {newMember?}
│ hall' = hall
│ outcome! = success
└────────────────────────────────
```

ClubState has been included instead of explicitly writing all the 'before' state declarations and predicates, to make the schema a little more succinct. Note the difference between this and Δ *ClubState* or Ξ *ClubState*.

The precondition schema pre *SuccessAddMember* is the schema

$SuccessAddMember \setminus (badminton', hall', outcome!)$

defined as follows:

```
┌──────── pre SuccessAddMember ──────────────────
│ ClubState
│ newMember? : STUDENT
├────────────────────────────────────────────────
│ ∃ badminton', hall' : ℙ STUDENT; outcome! : MESSAGE •
│   hall' ⊆ badminton'
│   ∧ # hall' ⩽ maxPlayers
│   ∧ newMember? ∉ badminton
│   ∧ badminton' = badminton ∪ {newMember?}
│   ∧ hall' = hall
│   ∧ outcome! = success
└────────────────────────────────────────────────
```

This can be simplified as follows:

$$hall' = hall$$

implies that we can remove the quantification of *hall'* and replace all references to *hall'* with *hall*. Furthermore

$$\exists\, outcome! : MESSAGE \bullet outcome! = success$$

is trivially true, and so can be removed, to give the following:

```
┌──────── pre SuccessAddMember ──────────
│ ClubState
│ newMember? : STUDENT
├────────────────────────────────────────
│ ∃ badminton' : ℙ STUDENT •
│   hall ⊆ badminton'
│   ∧ # hall ⩽ maxPlayers
│   ∧ newMember? ∉ badminton
│   ∧ badminton' = badminton ∪ {newMember?}
│   ∧ hall = hall
└────────────────────────────────────────
```

$$hall = hall$$

is trivially true, and can be removed.

$$\# \, hall \leqslant maxPlayers$$

is simply repeating the 'before' state invariant which we already have included with *ClubState*.

Now

$$badminton' = badminton \cup \{newMember?\}$$

and

$$hall \subseteq badminton \quad \text{(from } ClubState)$$

implies

$$hall \subseteq badminton'$$

Therefore the latter is unnecessary.

$$\exists\, badminton' : \mathbb{P}\ STUDENT \bullet badminton' = badminton \cup \{newMember?\}$$

is also trivially true, so the schema simplifies to

```
┌─ pre SuccessAddMember ──
│ ClubState
│ newMember? : STUDENT
├─────────────────────────
│ newMember? ∉ badminton
└─────────────────────────
```

We have arrived at the original precondition specified in the operation schema. This seems like a lot of work for no gain, but the preconditions of an operation are not always obvious from first inspection of the operation schema. The above precondition was explicitly stated in the operation schema, but it is possible to specify preconditions implicitly, in which case the above process would make them explicit. For example, if we are not interested in producing exception messages for the *AddMember* operation, we could leave out the predicate

$$newMember? \notin badminton$$

altogether.

```
┌──────── AddMember ──────────────────
│ Δ ClubState
│ newMember? : STUDENT
├──────────────────────────────────────
│ badminton' = badminton ∪ {newMember?}
│ hall' = hall
└──────────────────────────────────────
```

The operation has no effect when $newMember? \notin badminton$, and therefore does not violate the state invariant. However,

$newMember? \notin badminton$

is still implicitly the precondition for successfully adding a new member. Relying on implicit preconditions, which are implied by the operation's postconditions, or which arise as a consequence of the state invariant, is not necessarily wrong. You should always try to write specifications using whatever style is appropriate to make the specification clear, precise and understandable. However, it is still important to establish the conditions in which each operation is applicable, and that it has been correctly specified, and this often means explicitly calculating preconditions.

Exercise 4.6

For the *EnterHall* schema

```
┌─────── EnterHall ────────
│ Δ ClubState
│ enterer? : STUDENT
├──────────────────────────
│ enterer? ∈ badminton
│ enterer? ∉ hall
│ # hall < maxPlayers
│ hall' = hall ∪ {enterer?}
│ badminton' = badminton
└──────────────────────────
```

which of the explicitly stated preconditions could be made implicit? Write down the precondition schema for *EnterHall*.

Calculating preconditions can also reveal whether an operation is under-specified. For example, there may be combinations of 'before' state and inputs for which the operation does not specify anything. Take the *TotalAddMember* schema, for example.

$$TotalAddMember \mathrel{\hat{=}} (AddMember \wedge SuccessMessage) \vee IsMember$$
$$\mathrel{\hat{=}} SuccessAddMember \vee IsMember$$

We can take advantage of the fact that pre distributes through disjunction, that is

$$\text{pre } TotalAddMember = \text{pre } SuccessAddMember \vee \text{pre } IsMember$$

We have already calculated the pre *SuccessAddMember* schema above.

Expanding the *IsMember* schema, making all 'after' state declarations and predicates explicit, we get the following:

```
┌─── IsMember ────────
│ ClubState
│ badminton' : ℙ STUDENT
│ hall' : ℙ STUDENT
│ newMember? : STUDENT
│ outcome! : MESSAGE
├──────────────────────
│ hall' ⊆ badminton'
│ # hall' ⩽ maxPlayers
│
│ newMember? ∈ badminton
│ outcome! = isMember
│ badminton' = badminton
│ hall' = hall
└──────────────────────
```

Again, *ClubState* has been included instead of explicitly writing all the 'before' state declarations and predicates.

The precondition schema pre *IsMember* is the schema

$$IsMember \setminus (badminton', hall', outcome!)$$

defined as follows:

```
┌─── pre IsMember ──────────────────────────
│ ClubState
│ newMember? : STUDENT
├───────────────────────────────────────────
│ ∃ badminton', hall' : ℙ STUDENT; outcome! : MESSAGE •
│    hall' ⊆ badminton'
│    ∧ # hall' ⩽ maxPlayers
│    ∧ newMember? ∈ badminton
│    ∧ outcome! = isMember
│    ∧ badminton' = badminton
│    ∧ hall' = hall
└───────────────────────────────────────────
```

By a similar process to that used for pre *SuccessAddMember*, this schema simplifies to

$$\begin{array}{|l}
\underline{\quad}\ \text{pre } IsMember \ \underline{\quad} \\
ClubState \\
newMember?: STUDENT \\
\hline
newMember? \in badminton \\
\end{array}$$

which means that pre *TotalAddMember* is the schema

$$\begin{array}{|l}
\underline{\quad}\ \text{pre } TotalAddMember \ \underline{\quad} \\
ClubState \\
newMember?: STUDENT \\
\hline
newMember? \notin badminton \\
\quad \lor\ newMember? \in badminton \\
\end{array}$$

Clearly, the predicate simplifies to *true*, indicating that the operation is applicable for any combination of 'before' state and inputs. This confirms that the operation is indeed total.

4.14 In conclusion

In this chapter, we have met many of the fundamental techniques and notations used in writing Z specifications. In the rest of the book, we will introduce further mathematical structures and associated operators required to construct more sophisticated specifications, but the basic principles introduced here of modelling state and operations, and of structuring by means of the schema calculus, apply to most Z specifications.

Exercises 4.7

A simple computer game is to be based on the following description;

> The system consists of a pond which may contain any number of fish up to and including a given maximum. Conceptually, the user is fishing in the pond with a rod and line. The user has a net suspended in the pond into which s/he must place any fish which s/he catches.

For a Z specification of this system, we require the following basic type:

[*FISH*]   the set of all fish

and the following global description:

maxFish: $\mathbb{N}$ the maximum number of fish which the pond can contain.

1. Write a schema to describe the state of this system. Hint: At this level of abstraction, we are interested only in the pond, the net and the relationship between them.
2. Write a schema for an operation whereby the user catches a fish and places it in the net.
3. Write a schema for an operation whereby the user returns one or more fish to freedom in the pond.
4. Write a schema for an operation whereby a number of new fish are added to the pond.
5. Write a schema for an operation which outputs the number of fish which are currently free in the pond.

CHAPTER 5

A first specification:
The student badminton club

Aims

To describe the process of specification development, to outline a format for presenting specifications, and to present a complete simple specification.

Learning objectives

When you have completed this chapter, you should be able to:

- develop simple Z specifications in a methodical way;
- produce a well-organised specification document.

5.1 Introduction

In the previous chapter, we introduced many of the concepts necessary for writing Z specifications, illustrating them by reference to a simple specification. However, we did not fully describe a *method* to be used when developing a Z specification. Such a method must embrace both mechanisms for structuring a specification, as described in the previous chapter, and a process to be followed in the development of the specification.

5.2 The process of specification development

A methodical approach to the development of Z specifications has evolved from the work of the Programming Research Group at Oxford University, and others. This was referred to as 'The Established Strategy' by Barden *et al.* (1994), and a summary of some of the steps they suggest is given below. The structure of the specification document should also be based on this sequence. The document should contain both the formal Z text and accompanying informal text which provides explanations of the formal text and describes any aspects of the specification not amenable to formal description.

Firstly, *requirements analysis* is carried out, in which the sets and constants necessary to describe the important parts of the problem are identified.

Then the *basic types* of the specification are identified and recorded, together with any *global variables* required.

Next, the *state schema* is developed. For a complex state, several schemas may be used for its constituent parts, and combined using the schema calculus.

The *initial state* is then described, and a *proof* that this initial state exists.

This is followed by schemas describing the *operations*, without taking into consideration the error cases for each operation.

Next, the *preconditions* of the operations are calculated, and each operation schema is checked and, if necessary, modified to ensure that it explicitly contains its precondition predicate. This facilitates the construction of *error handling schemas*, usually one for each possible exception to the operation's preconditions.

For each operation, the successful case schema and the error schema(s) are now combined using schema disjunction to produce *total specifications* for each operation. However, if more than one error occurs simultaneously, the operation may be non-deterministic in that it does not specify which of the errors are to be reported. This could be overcome by including error messages not just for every individual error condition, but also for all combinations of error conditions. However, this would become extremely tedious and lead to unnecessarily large specifications. A better solution is to leave the non-determinism in the formal text and document it in the accompanying informal text, leaving it up to the implementor of the specification to decide how to handle multiple error conditions.

The above is a 'standalone' strategy for developing Z specifications. Various schemes have also been developed for integrating Z into the process of non-formal structured analysis methods such as SSADM and Yourdon, and several object-oriented versions of Z (Stepney *et al.* 1992) have been produced, but these topics are beyond the scope of this book.

5.3 The student badminton club specification

This specification is for a system to manage a student badminton club. The specification could be implemented as a computer system or paper records. The system will keep track of the whereabouts of the club members and add or remove members from the club.

Basic type and global variable

The student badminton club has the sole use of a hall with a single badminton court. To use the hall, one must be a member of the club. To ensure that everyone gets enough games, there is a limit of 20 people allowed in the hall at any one time.

The basic type required is as follows:

[STUDENT]   the set of all students

The limit on the number of people allowed in the hall is *maxPlayers*.

$$maxPlayers : \mathbb{N}$$
$$\rule{4cm}{0.4pt}$$
$$maxPlayers = 20$$

The state schema

ClubState
$$badminton : \mathbb{P}\ STUDENT$$
$$hall : \mathbb{P}\ STUDENT$$
$$\rule{4cm}{0.4pt}$$
$$hall \subseteq badminton$$
$$\# \ hall \leqslant maxPlayers$$

We are interested in the whereabouts of the members of the badminton club. We represent this information using two sets of students: *badminton*, the set of all members of the club, and *hall*, the set of all those who are in the hall. The invariant properties are:

1. A person in the hall must be a member of the club.

    $$hall \subseteq badminton$$

2. The number of people in the hall must not exceed *maxPlayers*.

    $$\# \ hall \leqslant maxPlayers$$

The initial state

For the initial state, there are no members in the club; that is, the sets *badminton* and *hall* are empty.

InitClubState
$$ClubState'$$
$$\rule{4cm}{0.4pt}$$
$$badminton' = \{\}$$
$$hall' = \{\}$$

We are obliged to verify that this is a valid state; that is, the state invariant property is not violated. A brief inspection in this case confirms that this is so, because

$$\{\,\} \subseteq \{\,\}$$

and

$$\forall\, n : \mathbb{N} \bullet \#\{\,\} \leqslant n$$

The operations

We now define the successful cases of operations to add or remove a member to/from the club, and to add or remove a member to/from the hall.

Adding a new member

To join the club, a potential member *newMember*? must register with the club secretary, after which the member may go to the hall to play. *newMember*? must not already be a member of the club, and joins the club outside the hall.

```
 _____ AddMember _____
| Δ ClubState
| newMember? : STUDENT
|_____
| newMember? ∉ badminton
| badminton' = badminton ∪ {newMember?}
| hall' = hall
|_____
```

Removing a member

This operation removes a member from the club. The operation is non-deterministic in that the member may or may not be inside the hall prior to the operation.

```
 _____ RemoveMember _____
| Δ ClubState
| member? : STUDENT
|_____
| member? ∈ badminton
| badminton' = badminton \ {member?}
| hall' = hall \ {member?}
|_____
```

Entering the hall

We now specify an operation for a student, *enterer?*, to enter the hall. The student must be a member of the club and must not already be in the hall, and the number of members already in the hall must be less than *maxPlayers*.

```
┌─────── EnterHall ───────
│ Δ ClubState
│ enterer? : STUDENT
├──────────────────────────
│ enterer? ∈ badminton
│ enterer? ∉ hall
│ # hall < maxPlayers
│ hall' = hall ∪ {enterer?}
│ badminton' = badminton
└──────────────────────────
```

Leaving the hall

We now specify an operation which removes a member from the hall. The member must be in the hall prior to the operation.

```
┌─────── LeaveHall ───────
│ Δ ClubState
│ leaver? : STUDENT
├──────────────────────────
│ leaver? ∈ hall
│ hall' = hall \ {leaver?}
│ badminton' = badminton
└──────────────────────────
```

Error handling schemas

The following free type represents the set of output messages required to construct total versions of the above operations, and for reports from the query operations which are defined below.

$$MESSAGE ::= success \mid isMember \mid notMember \mid hallFull \mid inHall \mid notInHall$$

The *success* message is used to indicate that an operation has been successfully completed, using the following schema:

$$SuccessMessage \cong [outcome! : MESSAGE \mid outcome! = success]$$

The precondition for the *AddMember* operation is

$newMember? \notin badminton$

The exception to this operation occurs if *newMember?* is already a member of the club. In this case, the state does not change and the message *isMember* is produced. This is specified by the following schema:

```
┌─── IsMember ──────────
│ Ξ ClubState
│ newMember? : STUDENT
│ outcome! : MESSAGE
├──────────────────────
│ newMember? ∈ badminton
│ outcome! = isMember
└──────────────────────
```

The precondition for the *RemoveMember* operation is

$member? \in badminton$

The exception to this operation occurs if *member?* is not a member of the club. In this case, the state does not change and the message *notMember* is produced. This is specified by the following schema:

```
┌─── NotMember ──────
│ Ξ ClubState
│ member? : STUDENT
│ outcome! : MESSAGE
├──────────────────────
│ member? ∉ badminton
│ outcome! = notMember
└──────────────────────
```

There are three preconditions for the *EnterHall* operation:

$enterer? \in badminton$
$enterer? \notin hall$
$\# hall < maxPlayers$

There are therefore three corresponding exceptions for this operation, namely

The person is not a member of the club
The person is already in the hall
The hall is already full to its designated capacity

For the first of these, we can use the *NotMember* schema defined above, with the appropriate renaming of the input:

NotMember [*enterer?* / *member?*]

The two other exceptions are specified by the following schemas:

```
┌──── AlreadyInHall ──────
│ Ξ ClubState
│ enterer? : STUDENT
│ outcome! : MESSAGE
├─────────────────────────
│ enterer? ∈ hall
│ outcome! = inHall
└─────────────────────────
```

```
┌────── HallFull ─────────
│ Ξ ClubState
│ outcome! : MESSAGE
├─────────────────────────
│ # hall = maxPlayers
│ outcome! = hallFull
└─────────────────────────
```

The exception to the *LeaveHall* schema occurs when the person is not in the hall. This is handled by the following schema. Note that we have chosen not to report the error condition where the person is not only not in the hall, but also not in the club. The corresponding precondition

leaver? ∈ *badminton*

is implicit in the operation schema.

```
┌──── NotInHall ──────────
│ Ξ ClubState
│ leaver? : STUDENT
│ outcome! : MESSAGE
├─────────────────────────
│ leaver? ∉ hall
│ outcome! = notInHall
└─────────────────────────
```

The total versions of the operation schemas are now defined using the above exception handling schemas.

$TotalAddMember \cong (AddMember \land SuccessMessage)$
$\lor IsMember$

$TotalRemoveMember \cong (RemoveMember \land SuccessMessage)$
$\lor NotMember$

$TotalEnterHall \cong (EnterHall \land SuccessMessage)$
$\lor NotMember \; [enterer? \,/\, member?]$
$\lor AlreadyInHall$
$\lor HallFull$

$TotalLeaveHall \cong (LeaveHall \land SuccessMessage)$
$\lor NotInHall$

Query operations

The following schema specifies an operation to output the set of all club members not in the hall:

```
┌─── OutsideHall ──────────
│ Ξ ClubState
│ outside! : ℙ STUDENT
├──────────────────────────
│ outside! = badminton \ hall
└──────────────────────────
```

There is no precondition; this operation may be applied to any state, and therefore no exception handling is necessary.

The following schema specifies an operation which inputs a student and outputs a message stating whether s/he is:

1. in the hall;
2. a member but not in the hall;
3. not a member.

```
┌─── Location ─────────────────────────────
│ Ξ ClubState
│ s? : STUDENT
│ report! : MESSAGE
├───────────────────────────────────────────
│ s? ∈ hall ⇒ report! = inHall
│ s? ∈ badminton ∧ s? ∉ hall ⇒ report! = notInHall
│ s? ∉ badminton ⇒ report! = notMember
└───────────────────────────────────────────
```

Again, there is no precondition, and therefore no exception handling is necessary.

CHAPTER 6

Relations

Aims

To introduce relations, to describe the operators associated with relations, and to illustrate the use of relations in constructing specifications.

Learning objectives

When you have completed this chapter, you should be able to:

- appreciate the importance of relations as a central feature of most Z specifications;
- recognise those parts of an informally described system which are appropriate for modelling with relations;
- select appropriate Z operators for specifying state invariant properties and operation pre- and postconditions involving relations;
- read and understand Z specifications involving relations, and provide informed criticism of them in respect of clarity and fitness for purpose.

6.1 Introduction

We have seen that the state of many simple systems can be represented by one or more sets of atomic items, with appropriate constraints. However, the specification of most systems of interest requires more sophisticated mathematical structures. In particular, we may wish to represent the information that there is a connection, or relationship, between some of the objects in our specification; for example, that two people are siblings or that one or more students are studying one or more modules. We can represent this sort of information using a new type of set called a *relation*. Let's look at some of the fundamental mathematical ideas that we need.

6.2 Ordered pairs, Cartesian product and relations

An *ordered pair* (a, b) consists of two elements: a is the first element and b is the second element. In Z, ordered pairs are represented by the *maplet* notation $a \mapsto b$. The *Cartesian product* $A \times B$ of sets A and B is the set of all the ordered pairs which can be formed such that the first element in each pair is a member of A and the second element in each pair is a member of B.

$$A \times B = \{a : A, b : B \bullet a \mapsto b\}$$

For example, given

$$A = \{1, 2\}$$
$$B = \{a, b, c\}$$

We have that

$$A \times B = \{1 \mapsto a, 1 \mapsto b, 1 \mapsto c, 2 \mapsto a, 2 \mapsto b, 2 \mapsto c\}$$

Note that $\#(A \times B) = \#A * \#B$.

The operator $\times$ is another means of constructing new types from existing ones; that is, if A and B are types, then $A \times B$ is a type, the elements of which are maplets.

A *binary relation* between two sets A and B is any subset of $A \times B$. Thus the declaration of a variable R which is a binary relation between sets A and B is given by

$$R : \mathbb{P}(A \times B)$$

In other words, R is a member of the powerset of the Cartesian product of A and B. The Z shorthand for this declaration is

$$R : A \leftrightarrow B$$

In the special case in which A and B are the same set, the relation is said to be *homogeneous*.

Note that if A and B are not types, then the type of R must be inferred from the types of A and B, as before.

Given the types

[*PERSON, CAT*]   the set of all people and the set of all cats respectively

the relation

$$owns = \{cathy \mapsto tiddles, susan \mapsto puss, harry \mapsto tiger\}$$

is a relation of type

$$PERSON \leftrightarrow CAT$$

The relation

$$R = \{1 \mapsto 5, 4 \mapsto 4, 1 \mapsto 8, 7 \mapsto 2\}$$

is a homogeneous relation of type $\mathbb{Z} \leftrightarrow \mathbb{Z}$.

To indicate that a maplet $a \mapsto b$ is a member of a binary relation R we can either use the conventional set membership operator, that is

$$a \mapsto b \in R$$

or use the name of the relation as an infix operator, that is

$$a \, R \, b$$

In either case, the meaning is that a is related to b by R. For example, for the above relation R the following are both true:

$$1 \mapsto 5 \in R$$
$$1 \, R \, 8$$

Note that the concept of Cartesian product may be generalised to more than two sets. Thus

$$A \times B \times C$$

defines the set of all triples (a, b, c) such that $a \in A$, $b \in B$, $c \in C$. In general, if there are n sets in the product, then the product set is a set of n-tuples (a 2-tuple is a pair, a 3-tuple is a triple, a 4-tuple is a quadruple).

Exercise 6.1

Given $A = \{1\}$, $B = \{2, 3\}$, write down the sets:

(i) $A \times B$
(ii) $\mathbb{P}(A) \times B$
(iii) $\mathbb{P}(A \times B)$
(iv) $(A \times B) \times (A \times B)$

6.3 The university modular degree scheme

A university operates a modular degree scheme, wherein students choose a selection of modules from a large menu. (There are certain restrictions on their choices, discussion of which we will defer until later.) One function of the administration system for the scheme is to keep track of which students are doing which modules. We define the basic types

$[PERSON, MODULE]$ the set of all people and the set of all modules respectively

Then the type

$$PERSON \times MODULE = \{p : PERSON, m : MODULE \bullet p \mapsto m\}$$

is the set of all ordered pairs (maplets) such that the first thing in each pair is a person and the second thing in each pair is a module. We will consider the maplet $p \mapsto m$ to represent the information that person p is taking module m. The information for the entire modular degree scheme would therefore be represented by a *set* of maplets, that is by a relation which is a subset of $PERSON \times MODULE$. We will call this relation

$taking : PERSON \leftrightarrow MODULE$

Exercises 6.2

1. What relation would represent a degree scheme where none of the people are taking any of the modules?
2. What relation would represent a degree scheme where every person in the world is taking every possible module?
3. Given the set

    $firstYear : \mathbb{P}\ PERSON$

    the set of all first-year students, define the set of all first-year students who are taking the module *programming*.

6.4 Source, target, domain and range of a relation

Suppose the relation *taking* has the value

$\{Alice \mapsto C++,\ Chris \mapsto C++,\ Chris \mapsto Z,\ Sandra \mapsto Z,\ Sandra \mapsto Database\}$

We can represent this relation as a picture as shown in Figure 6.1.

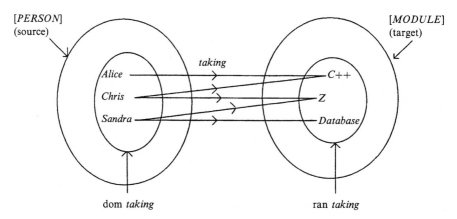

Figure 6.1   The relation *taking*

The types (maximal sets) *PERSON* and *MODULE* named in the declaration of the relation *taking* are sometimes called the *source* and *target* sets respectively. The source is the set from which the first element of each maplet in a given relation must be drawn, and the target is the set from which the second element in each maplet in a given relation must be drawn. Each maplet in the relation *taking* is represented by an arrow in Figure 6.1.

The *domain* of the relation *taking*, referred to in Z as dom *taking*, is that subset of the source set whose members have at least one arrow coming out of them. In other words, the set of all people who occur as the first element of at least one of the maplets in *taking*.

$$\text{dom } taking = \{ p : PERSON, \, m : MODULE \mid p \mapsto m \in taking \bullet p \}$$

For the above example

$$\text{dom } taking = \{Alice, \ Chris, \ Sandra\}$$

The *range* of *taking*, referred to as ran *taking*, is that subset of the target set whose members have at least one arrow entering them; in other words the set of all modules which occur as the second element of at least one of the maplets in *taking*.

$$\text{ran } taking = \{ p : PERSON, \, m : MODULE \mid p \mapsto m \in taking \bullet m \}$$

For the above example

$$\text{ran } taking = \{C++, \ Z, \ Database\}$$

6.5 Module registration

Clearly, *taking* will be an important part of the representation of the state of our administration system. However, we are only interested in the set of people who are registered as students at the university, and the set of modules which are part of the modular degree scheme.

$students : \mathbb{P} \; PERSON$
$degModules : \mathbb{P} \; MODULE$

This places a restriction on the maplets allowed in the relation *taking*. The people doing modules must be registered as students, and the modules they are doing must be bona fide degree modules at our university.

$\text{dom } taking \subseteq students$
$\text{ran } taking \subseteq degModules$

One of the good things about Z is that using it makes us focus on the problem – to concentrate on precisely what we are trying to specify. A good notation cannot make us write correct specifications, but it does make it more *likely* that we will. We write something down in the Z notation; it only has one meaning, and in considering what we have written down we must confront the question of what it was that we were trying to say, or should have been trying to say, in the first place. At this stage, we might consider issues such as:

- is every student taking one or more modules?
- does every module have students taking it?
- can a student be registered for more than one course (different named degrees within the modular scheme, or HND and HNC courses)?
- are the sets of modules for each course disjoint?

For simplicity, we choose not to consider other courses within the university, but we do allow the possibility that a student registered on the degree scheme may not be doing any modules (the student may be intermitting, that is taking a break from the course, or may be on a sandwich placement), and that a module within the scheme may not have any students. The schema describing the state of the module registration part of the administration system is thus

$$
\begin{array}{|l}
\quad\underline{\quad ModuleReg \quad}\underline{\qquad\qquad} \\
students : \mathbb{P} \; PERSON \\
degModules : \mathbb{P} \; MODULE \\
taking : PERSON \leftrightarrow MODULE \\
\hline
\text{dom } taking \subseteq students \\
\text{ran } taking \subseteq degModules \\
\end{array}
$$

Note that because relations are sets, all the set operations that we have met so far (union, intersection, membership, etc.) may be applied to them. In fact, in this and the following chapters, we will be considering a hierarchy of different types of sets, each of which is a more restricted form of its predecessor, and each of which is associated with successively richer sets of operations, comprising those operations 'inherited' from the predecessors together with new operations specific to that structure. Thus relations are a special type of set, functions (Chapter 7) are a special type of relation, and sequences (Chapter 9) are a special type of function.

Exercises 6.3

1. Give a Z expression for the set of all students who are not taking any modules.
2. Give a Z expression for the set of all degree modules which have no students.
3. Suppose that there is a maximum of n people allowed to study a module. Give a Z expression for the set of all modules which are full; that is, which have precisely n people taking them.
4. Write down the additional predicate required in the schema *ModuleReg*, to incorporate the maximum limit of n people described at 3 above.
5. Give an appropriate type for a variable *matches*, which represents the draw for a round in a tennis tournament. What invariant predicates would have to be associated with *matches* to ensure that each person in the draw is only in one match, and is not playing against themselves?

6.6 Relational image

Given a relation $R: A \leftrightarrow B$ and a set $S \subseteq A$, the *relational image* of S in R is defined as follows:

$$R(S) = \{b : B \mid \exists a : A \bullet a \in S \land a \mapsto b \in R\}$$

In other words, the set of all those members of ran R that are related by R to members of S.

For example, the set of all modules being studied by student p is

$taking\,(\{p\})$

For the value of *taking* shown in Figure 6.1

$taking\,(\{Alice,\ Chris\}) = \{C++,\ Z\}$

6.7 Inverse of a relation

Given a relation $R: A \leftrightarrow B$, the *inverse* of R is defined as

$$R^{-1} == \{a: A, b: B \mid a \mapsto b \in R \bullet b \mapsto a\}$$

In other words, R^{-1} is the relation obtained by reversing the order of each of the maplets in R, or to put it another way, by reversing the direction of all the arrows in the picture of R. The *type* of the inverse relation is therefore

$$R^{-1}: B \leftrightarrow A$$

For example, for the value of *taking* shown in Figure 6.1 we have

$$taking^{-1} = \{C{+}{+} \mapsto Alice, \; C{+}{+} \mapsto Chris, \; Z \mapsto Chris, \; Z \mapsto Sandra,$$
$$Database \mapsto Sandra\}$$

Exercises 6.4

1. Write a Z expression for the set of all students taking module m.
2. Write a Z expression for the set of all students who are taking at least one module which student s is taking.
3. Write an alternative answer to question 4 of Exercises 6.3, using relational image and inverse.

6.8 Operations

We will now consider the successful cases of some of the operations which the university's administration staff will wish to perform on this part of the system state. As before, some of these will cause the state to change and some will simply interrogate the state for information.

Adding a new student to the university

For a person $p?$ to become a student at the university, the precondition is that s/he is not one already!

```
_____ AddStudent _____
Δ ModuleReg
p?: PERSON
─────────────────────
p? ∉ students
students' = students ∪ {p?}
degModules' = degModules
taking' = taking
```

Registering a student for a module

In order that a person *p*? may become registered for a module *m*? we require that:

1. *p*? is a student at the university.
2. *m*? is a valid module in the degree scheme.
3. *p*? is not already registered for *m*?.

We can add the maplet $p? \mapsto m?$ to the relation *taking* by placing it in a singleton set and taking the union of this set with *taking*. This technique is very commonly used when writing operation specifications using relations. The schema is as follows:

```
┌─────── RegForModule ───────
│ Δ ModuleReg
│ p? : PERSON
│ m? : MODULE
├─────────────────────────────
│ p? ∈ students
│ m? ∈ degModules
│ p? ↦ m? ∉ taking
│ taking' = taking ∪ {p? ↦ m?}
│ students' = students
│ degModules' = degModules
└─────────────────────────────
```

Exercises 6.5

1. Write Z schemas for operations to:

   (i)   remove a student from the university;
   (ii) withdraw a student from a module (Hint: Use the set difference operator \.);
   (iii) add a new module to the degree scheme;
   (iv) remove a module from the degree scheme.

2. Let there be a limit of *n* students who may be registered for any single module. Modify the *RegForModule* schema to take account of this extra constraint, and use the schema calculus to define a total version of this operation, that is one which deals appropriately with all possible exceptions to the schema preconditions.

6.9 Domain and range restriction and anti-restriction

Given a relation $R: A \leftrightarrow B$ and a set $S \subseteq A$, R *domain restricted* to S may be defined as follows:

$$S \lhd R = \{a \mapsto b : A \times B \mid a \mapsto b \in R \wedge a \in S\}$$

In other words, $S \lhd R$ defines a relation which is the result of removing from R all maplets with first elements that are not members of S. For example, suppose we have the set *firstYear* $\subseteq$ *students*, the set of all students in the first year of their degree course. The subset of *taking* which relates just first-year students to the modules they are taking is given by

firstYear $\lhd$ *taking*

The operation of domain restriction is complemented by that of domain anti-restriction. *R domain anti-restricted* to S may be defined as follows:

$$S \ntriangleleft R = \{a \mapsto b : A \times B \mid a \mapsto b \in R \wedge a \notin S\}$$

In other words, $S \ntriangleleft R$ defines a relation which is the result of removing from R all maplets with first elements that *are* members of S. For example, the subset of *taking* which relates all degree students that are not in their first year to the modules they are taking is

firstYear $\ntriangleleft$ *taking*

The above operators restrict a relation to those maplets whose *first element* is or is not a member of a given set. We can also define similar operators which restrict a relation to those maplets whose *second element* is or is not a member of a given set, namely *range* restriction and anti-restriction respectively. Given the relation R as above and the set $T \subseteq B$, then *R range restricted* to T may be defined as follows:

$$R \rhd T = \{a \mapsto b : A \times B \mid a \mapsto b \in R \wedge b \in T\}$$

In other words, $R \rhd T$ defines a relation which is the result of removing from R all maplets with second elements which are not members of T. Finally, *R range anti-restricted* to T may be defined as follows:

$$R \ntriangleright T = \{a \mapsto b : A \times B \mid a \mapsto b \in R \wedge b \notin T\}$$

In other words, $R \ntriangleright T$ defines a relation which is the result of removing from R all maplets with second elements which *are* members of T. For example, suppose we have the set

progMods $\subseteq$ *degModules*

the set of all modules which involve programming. The subset of *taking* which relates students to just their modules which involve programming is

$$taking \rhd progMods$$

and the subset of *taking* which relates students to just their modules which don't involve programming is

$$taking \ \rhd\!\!\!- progMods$$

As a further example, suppose the relation *taking* has the value given in Section 6.4 above.

$$taking = \{Alice \mapsto C++, \ Chris \mapsto C++, \ Chris \mapsto Z, \ Sandra \mapsto Z,$$
$$Sandra \mapsto Database\}$$

Then the following are all true:

$$\{Alice, \ Chris\} \lhd taking = \{Alice \mapsto C++, \ Chris \mapsto C++, \ Chris \mapsto Z\}$$
$$\{Alice, \ Chris\} \ \lhd\!\!\!- taking = \{Sandra \mapsto Z, \ Sandra \mapsto Database\}$$
$$taking \rhd \{Z\} = \{Chris \mapsto Z, \ Sandra \mapsto Z\}$$
$$taking \ \rhd\!\!\!- \{Z, \ C++\} = \{Sandra \mapsto Database\}$$

Exercises 6.6

1. Given the relation

    $$R = \{1 \mapsto 1, 2 \mapsto 4, 3 \mapsto 9, 4 \mapsto 16, 5 \mapsto 25\}$$

    and the set $S = \{1, 4, 5\}$, simplify the value of each of the following expressions:
    (i) $S \lhd R$
    (ii) $R \rhd S$
    (iii) $S \lhd R \rhd S$
    (iv) $(R \rhd dom \ R)^{-1} \rhd S$

2. Given the set *firstYear* as above, write down two ways to describe in Z the set of all modules which first-year students are taking. (Note that for many problems there is more than one reasonable way to specify a solution. Trying to think of alternative solutions to any given problem will improve your familiarity with the notation and its application.)
3. Given the set *progMods* as above, write down a Z expression for the set of all students who aren't studying any programming.

4. Look back through the other exercises in this chapter and see whether they could have been answered using the restriction and anti-restriction operators.

6.10 Composition and transitive closure

The *forward composition* of relations $R : A \leftrightarrow B$ and $S : B \leftrightarrow C$ is denoted by

$$R \, ; S$$

and is the relation of type $A \leftrightarrow C$ defined as follows:

$$R \, ; S = \{a : A; c : C \mid (\exists b : B \bullet a \mapsto b \in R \wedge b \mapsto c \in S) \bullet a \mapsto c\}$$

The important point is that the target set of R is a subset of the source set of S. For example, let

$$A = \{1, 2, 3, 4\}$$
$$B = \{a, b, c, d\}$$
$$C = \{p, q, r, s\}$$

and

$$R = \{1 \mapsto a, 1 \mapsto b, 2 \mapsto b, 4 \mapsto d\}$$
$$S = \{a \mapsto p, b \mapsto q, c \mapsto q, c \mapsto r\}$$

Then

$$R \, ; S = \{1 \mapsto p, 1 \mapsto q, 2 \mapsto q\}$$

This is illustrated in Figure 6.2

Informally, a maplet $x \mapsto y$ is a member of $R \, ; S$ iff you can get from x to y in the picture by following two consecutive arrows.

If a relation is *homogeneous*, it can be composed with itself. For example, when someone writes an academic paper, they include a list of references, citing other papers, the content of which they have referred to in their own paper. Let the set of all academic papers be

$$[PAPER]$$

and let *cites*: $PAPER \leftrightarrow PAPER$ be the relation such that x *cites* y (where x and y are papers) has the obvious meaning. Then

$$x \; cites \, ; cites \; y$$

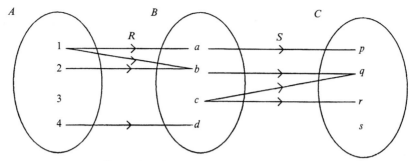

Figure 6.2 Composition of relations R and S

would mean that paper x cites a paper which cites paper y and

$$x \ cites\,;cites\,;cites \ y$$

would mean that x cites a paper which cites a paper which cites y, and so on. There is a shorthand notation to express such multiple composition, as follows. The *identity relation* on a set X is

$$\text{id}\,X = \{x : X \bullet x \mapsto x\}$$

that is, the relation which maps every element of X to itself. For a relation $R : X \leftrightarrow X$

$$R^0 = \text{id}\,X$$
$$R^1 = R$$
$$R^2 = R\,;R$$
$$R^3 = R\,;R\,;R$$
$$\vdots$$

The *transitive closure* of R, denoted by R^+, is the relation obtained by taking the union of all of these relations except R^0, that is

$$R^+ = \bigcup\{n : \mathbb{N} \mid n > 0 \bullet R^n\}$$

The *reflexive transitive closure* of R, denoted by R^*, is obtained by including R^0 in the union:

$$R^* = \bigcup\{n : \mathbb{N} \mid n \geqslant 0 \bullet R^n\} = R^+ \cup R^0$$

So $x \ cites^+ \ y$ means that x cites y either directly or indirectly via one or more other papers. In other words, there exists at least one sequence of papers, beginning with x and ending with y, in which each successive paper (except the last one) cites the next in the sequence. Here we are using the term 'sequence' in its informal sense. In Chapter 9 we will give a formal description of sequences, which are a powerful tool in writing Z specifications. Note that the relation *cites** would also relate every paper to itself, although such a citation is not normal practice in the academic community!

Exercises 6.7

1. Write a Z expression for the set of all papers cited directly or indirectly by paper x.
2. Write a Z expression for the set of all papers which cite other papers (directly or indirectly) but are not themselves cited (directly or indirectly).
3. Write a Z expression which states that if any paper cites another (directly or indirectly), then the second one may not cite the first (directly or indirectly).
4. The university also wishes to keep track of which modules each student has completed. Extend the state schema of the module registration system specification to incorporate this feature. You might also like to think about any new operations which would be necessary.
5. A student may not retake a module which s/he has already completed. Modify the schema which registers a student for a module to allow for this restriction.
6. In a modular degree scheme such as the one described above, some modules may only be taken if one or more prerequisite modules have been passed. Extend the state schema to incorporate a prerequisite structure. You may also wish to specify some operations for the new state, for example an operation to enquire which modules are prerequisite for a given module.

CHAPTER 7

Functions

Aims

To introduce the concept of the function as a specialised sort of relation, to introduce function operators and to show how functions may be used in Z specifications.

Learning objectives

When you have completed this chapter, you should be able to:

- recognise whether a given relation is a function, and whether a function is total, injective, surjective or bijective;
- decide where functions are needed within your specifications;
- understand and use the operators introduced earlier in this book, and those introduced in this chapter, in creating function-valued expressions.

7.1 Introduction

The concept of the function is a very useful and powerful one in computer science. Procedural programming languages such as C and Pascal support the use of functions as algorithms for transforming input parameters or arguments into output values. The functional programming paradigm, as represented by languages such as ML and Miranda, is based on the idea of constructing programs from side-effect-free functions. The expressive power of such languages facilitates the production of succinct, elegant, understandable and modifiable code. As we shall see, functions are also an extremely important tool in writing Z specifications.

7.2 Functions in Z

A function is a special sort of relation. A relation $f: A \leftrightarrow B$ is a *partial function* iff it satisfies the following condition:

$$\forall x: A; y, z: B \bullet x \mapsto y \in f \wedge x \mapsto z \in f \Rightarrow y = z$$

In other words, in the picture of f, there is *at most* one arrow emerging from each element of the source set, or to put it another way, there are no diverging arrows emerging from any element of dom f. Note that there is not necessarily an arrow emerging from every source set element. A partial function f is declared as

$$f: A \nrightarrow B$$

A *total function,* declared as

$$f: A \rightarrow B$$

is a partial function for which

$$\text{dom } f = A$$

that is, every source element has an arrow emerging. The use of the declarations $f: A \nrightarrow B$ and $f: A \rightarrow B$ is therefore a shorthand for the declaration $f: A \leftrightarrow B$ together with the appropriate predicates from above. This means that if f is part of a state schema, we must ensure that any state-changing operations do not violate these predicates, which are an implicit part of the state invariant. In other words, if we have declared an object as a total or partial function, it must remain one!

For a function f as above, if we have

$$x \mapsto y \in f$$

then we may write

$$fx = y$$

The notation fx is read as 'the function f applied to the argument x'. The concept is analogous to the notion of relational image discussed in the last chapter.

Exercises 7.1

The following types are given:

$cols ::= red \,|\, blue \,|\, green$
$plants ::= pansy \,|\, geranium$

1. State whether each of the following is a partial function, a total function or neither.

    (i) $f = \{red \mapsto geranium\}$
    (ii) $g = \{blue \mapsto pansy,\ blue \mapsto geranium\}$
    (iii) $h = \{red \mapsto pansy,\ blue \mapsto pansy,\ green \mapsto pansy\}$
    (iv) $i = \{\}$

2. What can you say about the type of h^{-1} (the inverse of h)?

3. The *backward composition* of relations $S : B \leftrightarrow C$ and $R : A \leftrightarrow B$ is denoted by $S \circ R$ and is the relation of type $A \leftrightarrow C$ defined as follows:

    $$S \circ R = \{a : A; c : C \,|\, (\exists b : B \bullet a \mapsto b \in R \wedge b \mapsto c \in S) \bullet a \mapsto c\}$$

    (i)   What is the relationship between $S \circ R$ and $R ; S$?
    (ii)   If R and S are functions, write down an alternative expression for $(S \circ R)x$.
    (iii) Given the function $double : \mathbb{N} \rightarrow \mathbb{N}$, where

    $$\forall x : \mathbb{N} \bullet double\ x = 2{*}x$$

    how would you describe the function $double \circ double$?

7.3 Function overriding

The overriding operator, $\oplus$, may be applied to any two functions f and g, of the same type, and the result is another function. The expression

$$f \oplus g$$

read as 'f overridden by g', defines a new function with the following properties:

$$\mathrm{dom}(f \oplus g) = \mathrm{dom}\,f \cup \mathrm{dom}\,g$$

$$\forall x : \mathrm{dom}(f \oplus g) \bullet ((x \in \mathrm{dom}\,g \Rightarrow (f \oplus g)x = gx)$$
$$\wedge (x \in \mathrm{dom}\,f \wedge x \notin \mathrm{dom}\,g \Rightarrow (f \oplus g)x = fx))$$

In other words, $f \oplus g$ behaves the same as f when applied to objects not in the domain of g, and behaves as g otherwise. The term 'overriding' refers to the fact that, when $f \oplus g$ is applied to objects in the intersection of the domains of f and g, it is the maplets from g which take precedence.

For example, let f and g be as follows:

$$f, g : \mathbb{N} \nrightarrow \mathbb{N}$$
$$f = \{3 \mapsto 9, 4 \mapsto 16, 5 \mapsto 25\}$$
$$g = \{2 \mapsto 7, 3 \mapsto 16, 4 \mapsto 17\}$$

This situation is illustrated in Figure 7.1

From Figure 7.1, we see that 3 is mapped to 9 by f and to 16 by g. Therefore 3 is mapped to 16 by $f \oplus g$. Similarly, 4 is mapped to 16 by f and to 17 by g. Therefore 4 is mapped to 17 by $f \oplus g$. The resultant function is therefore

$$f \oplus g = \{2 \mapsto 7, 3 \mapsto 16, 4 \mapsto 17, 5 \mapsto 25\}$$

This is illustrated in Figure 7.2.

As stated above, a function is a restricted sort of relation, which in turn is a restricted sort of set. This means that all the relation operators and set operators introduced in earlier chapters may be applied to functions, although as we discovered in Exercises 7.1 the result of such applications is not necessarily a function.

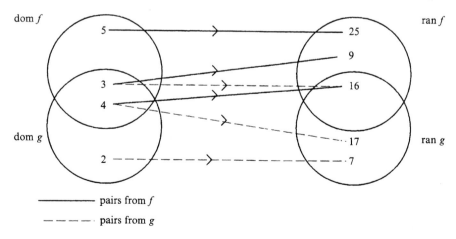

Figure 7.1 The functions f and g

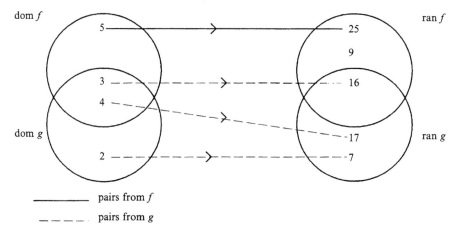

Figure 7.2 Function *f* overridden by function *g* (*f* ⊕ *g*)

Exercises 7.2

1. For the above functions *f* and *g*, what is the value of the following expressions?

    (i) $g \oplus f$
    (ii) $f^{-1} \oplus g^{-1}$
    (iii) $\{5\} \lhd f \oplus g \rhd \{17, 7\}$
    (iv) $f \cap g \oplus f \cup g$
    (v) $(f^{-1} ; g) \oplus g$

2. For *any* two functions *f* and *g*, in what circumstances could the following expressions be true?

    (i) $f \cup g = f \oplus g$
    (ii) $f \oplus g = g \oplus f$
    (iii) $f \cap g = f \oplus g$
    (iv) $f \setminus g = f \oplus g$

7.4 Restricted functions

We may specify that a function is to be restricted to satisfy some given property. Some of these restricted functions have names and special symbols in Z (variations of the arrow symbol defining a function type). However, they are not often required, and the symbols will not be listed here. The special functions are as follows.

A function $f: A \rightarrowtail B$ is an *injection* iff every value in ran f occurs in precisely one maplet in f. In other words, there are no converging arrows in the picture of f. An injective function is also called a *one-to-one* function. To specify that f has this property, we could include the following predicate in the schema in which f is defined:

$$\forall x, y: A; z: B \bullet fx = z \wedge fy = z \Rightarrow x = y$$

The function $f: A \twoheadrightarrow B$ is a *surjection* iff *every* value in B is mapped to by the function, that is

ran $f = B$

A surjective function is said to be *onto* its target.

The function $f: A \rightarrow B$ is a *bijection* iff f is an injection, a surjection and is total.

Exercises 7.3

1. Give an alternative predicate to specify that the function $f: A \twoheadrightarrow B$ is a surjection.
2. What can you say about the inverse of a function which is an injection?
3. What can you say about the inverse of a function which is a surjection?
4. What can you say about the inverse of a function which is a bijection?
5. We can define a global constant function in a specification using an *axiomatic description* which, you will recall from Chapter 4, is a Z construct for defining a global object. Describe the following function in English, and state which of the above properties it possesses.

$$
\begin{array}{|l}
f: \mathbb{Z} \rightarrow \mathbb{Z} \\
\hline
\forall x: \mathbb{Z} \bullet fx = x
\end{array}
$$

6. Give examples of functions of type $\mathbb{N} \twoheadrightarrow \mathbb{N}$ which are injections, surjections and/or bijections.
7. Recall the fishing game specification in Chapter 4, Exercises 4.7. Extend the state schema there to include a function which maps each fish in the pond to its weight rounded to the nearest whole number of grams. Write a schema to specify an operation to return the weight of the heaviest fish currently in the net.

A second specification: The video shop

8.1 Introduction and basic types

A video rental shop keeps one or more copies of each of a set of video titles. To rent a copy, a person must be registered with the shop as one of its members. For simplicity, we will say that a given member can only have one copy of any given title on rental at any given time. We identify the basic types in our specification as

[*PERSON*]   the set of all people
[*TITLE*]   the set of all video titles

Note that a title is an abstract idea; each physical video cassette is not a title, but a *copy* of a title.

8.2 The system state

The state of the system must contain all information relevant to our (albeit simplified) video shop: who the members are, which titles are stocked and how many copies of each, and which titles are currently rented out to which members.

We can capture this information in the following state schema:

```
┌─────── VideoShop ──────────────────────────
│ members : ℙ PERSON
│ rented : PERSON ↔ TITLE
│ stockLevel : TITLE ⇸ ℕ₁
├─────────────────────────────────────────────
│ dom rented ⊆ members
│ ran rented ⊆ dom stockLevel
│ ∀t : ran rented • # rented ▷ {t} ≤ stockLevel t
└─────────────────────────────────────────────
```

Here:

members is the set of all registered members.

$p \mapsto t \in rented$ iff person p currently has a copy of title t out on loan. *rented* is a relation, which captures the fact that each member can have copies of many video titles on loan (but only *one* copy of each title), and copies of each video title can be on loan to many people.

stockLevel t is the number of copies of title t stocked by the shop. *stockLevel* is a function because each title in dom *stockLevel* is associated with precisely one stock-level figure, and *stockLevel* is a partial function, because the shop does not necessarily stock all the titles in the world! The target of *stockLevel* is $\mathbb{N}_1$, which states that the stock level for any title in stock cannot be zero.

dom *stockLevel* is the set of titles stocked by the shop.

The predicate

    dom *rented* ⊆ *members*

captures the requirement that only members may rent videos.

The predicate

    ran *rented* ⊆ dom *stockLevel*

captures the requirement that a video can be rented iff it is in stock.

The predicate

    ∀t : ran *rented* • # *rented* ▷ {t} ≤ *stockLevel* t

captures the requirement that the shop cannot rent out more copies of a given title than it has in stock.

8.3 The initial state

In the initial state, there are no members and no stock.

```
┌─ InitVideoShop ──────────
│ VideoShop'
├──────────────────────────
│ members' = { }
│ stockLevel' = { }
└──────────────────────────
```

The only possible value of *rented'* is therefore the empty set, and the invariant

$$\forall t : \text{ran } rented' \bullet \# \, rented' \rhd \{t\} \leqslant stockLevel \, t$$

is trivially true, as ran *rented'* is the empty set. The initial state is therefore a valid state for the system.

8.4 Operations

We now specify the successful cases for operations to rent out a video, change the stock level of a given title, and remove a given title from stock. Each of these successful cases will cause a change in the system state. We then specify the successful cases of some query operations which interrogate but do not change the state. These comprise an operation to return the set of all titles rented by a given person, an operation to return the number of copies of a given title which are out on rental, and an operation to return the number of copies of a given title which are in the shop.

Renting out a video

This operation will change the state, and therefore includes Δ *VideoShop*. The inputs required are a person to rent the video and the title to be rented. There are no explicit outputs, only a change of state. The preconditions are as follows:

1. The person *p?* is a member, and the title *t?* is in stock.

    $p? \in members$
    $t? \in \text{dom } stockLevel$

2. At least one copy of title *t?* is available for renting.

    $stockLevel \, t? > \# \, rented \rhd \{t?\}$

3. The person does not already have a copy of title $t?$ on rental.

$p? \mapsto t? \notin rented$

The postcondition simply adds the required maplet to the relation *rented*.

$rented' = rented \cup \{p? \mapsto t?\}$

The operation schema is as follows:

$\begin{array}{|l}
\underline{\qquad RentVideo \qquad\qquad} \\
\Delta\ VideoShop \\
p? : PERSON \\
t? : TITLE \\
\hline
p? \in members \\
t? \in \text{dom } stockLevel \\
stockLevel\ t? > \#\ rented \rhd \{t?\} \\
p? \mapsto t? \notin rented \\
rented' = rented \cup \{p? \mapsto t?\} \\
stockLevel' = stockLevel \\
members' = members \\
\end{array}$

Increasing or decreasing the stock level of a given title

This operation requires the title and the required change in stock level (which may be positive or negative) as inputs. The preconditions are as follows:

1. The title $t?$ must be in stock.

    $t? \in \text{dom } stockLevel$

2. The potential change must leave a positive number of copies of the title in stock.

    $stockLevel\ t? + change? > 0$

3. The number of copies of the title in stock after the operation must not be less than the number of copies out on rental.

    $stockLevel\ t? + change? \geq \#\ rented \rhd \{t?\}$

The postcondition uses the overriding operator $\oplus$ to modify a single pair from *stockLevel* using a singleton function.

$$stockLevel' = stockLevel \oplus \{t? \mapsto stockLevel\ t? + change?\}$$

Title $t?$ is mapped by *stockLevel'* to the new value for its stock level. This is a very common pattern of usage for $\oplus$.

You should note that preconditions 2 and 3 are not strictly necessary. Precondition 2 is implicit in the postcondition, as the target of *stockLevel* is $\mathbb{N}_1$. Precondition 3 is implicit in the 'after' state invariant

$$\forall t : \text{ran } rented' \bullet \# rented' \rhd \{t\} \leqslant stockLevel'\ t$$

together with the postcondition. However, we include them in order to construct exception handling schemas for each of these conditions.

The operation schema is as follows:

```
┌─── ChangeStockLevel ──────────────────────
│ Δ VideoShop
│ t? : TITLE
│ change? : ℤ
├───────────────────────────────────────────
│ t? ∈ dom stockLevel
│ stockLevel t? + change? > 0
│ stockLevel t? + change? ⩾ # rented ⩾ {t?}
│ stockLevel' = stockLevel ⊕ {t? ↦ stockLevel t? + change?}
│ rented' = rented
│ members' = members
└───────────────────────────────────────────
```

Removing a title from stock

The title $t?$ must be in stock, and there must be no copies of the title out on rental.

$$t? \notin \text{ran } rented$$
$$t? \in \text{dom } stockLevel$$

We must remove the pair containing this title from the *stockLevel* function.

$$stockLevel' = \{t?\} \lhd stockLevel$$

This time, instead of using overriding to map $t?$ to a new range element, we have removed the pair from the function altogether, using the domain anti-restriction operator $\lhd$.

The operation schema is as follows:

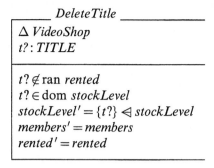

Note that the predicate

$$t? \in \text{dom } stockLevel$$

is not strictly necessary, because if $t?$ is not in the domain of $stockLevel$, the predicate

$$stockLevel' = \{t?\} \lhd stockLevel$$

represents no change in $stockLevel$. However, in the implementation of the system, we will want to pick this up as an exception to be reported to the user, and it is therefore included in the specification with an appropriate exception handling schema (see below) to specify the generation of a message when the title is not in stock.

Finding out the titles currently rented out by a given person

This operation will not change the state, and therefore includes Ξ *VideoShop*. The person must be a member. The required set of titles is the relational image in *rented* of the set containing only this person.

```
┌─── TitlesOut ──────
│ Ξ VideoShop
│ p? : PERSON
│ titles! : ℙ TITLE
├────────────────────
│ p? ∈ members
│ titles! = rented(|{ p? })
└────────────────────
```

The number of copies of a given title currently out on rental

The title must be one stocked by the shop. The required output is the number of pairs in *rented* which have this title as their second element.

```
┌───── CopiesRentedOut ───────
│ Ξ VideoShop
│ t? : TITLE
│ copiesOut! : ℕ
├────────────────────────────
│ t? ∈ dom stockLevel
│ copiesOut! = # rented ▷ {t?}
└────────────────────────────
```

The number of copies of a given title currently in the shop

The title must be one that is stocked by the shop. The required output is the number of copies stocked by the shop minus the number of copies currently out on rental. We can access the latter by including the *CopiesRentedOut* schema with appropriate renaming of *copiesOut!* so that it is not an output from the operation. Note that this also brings the declaration of the title *t?* and Ξ *VideoShop* into scope.

```
┌────── CopiesInShop ──────────────────────
│ CopiesRentedOut[copiesOut / copiesOut!]
│ copiesIn! : ℕ
├──────────────────────────────────────────
│ t? ∈ dom stockLevel
│ copiesIn! = stockLevel t? − copiesOut
└──────────────────────────────────────────
```

8.5 Error handling schemas

The following free type represents the set of output messages required to construct total versions of the above operations:

$$MESSAGE ::= success \mid notMember \mid notInStock \mid allCopiesOut$$
$$\mid alreadyRented \mid nonPosStockLevel \mid tooManyRented$$
$$\mid stillRented$$

The *success* message is used to indicate that an operation has been successfully completed, using the following schema:

$$SuccessMessage \; \hat{=} \; [outcome! : MESSAGE \mid outcome! = success]$$

Renting out a· video

The precondition exceptions and the schemas to handle them are as follows:

1. The person *p*? is not a member.

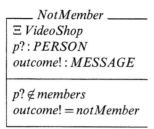

2. The title *t*? is not in stock.

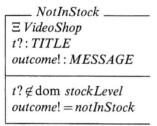

3. No copy of title *t*? is available.

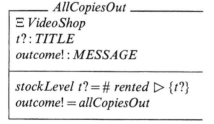

4. The person already has a copy on rental.

```
┌─── AlreadyRented ──────
│ Ξ VideoShop
│ p? : PERSON
│ t? : TITLE
│ outcome! : MESSAGE
├──────────────────────────
│ p? ↦ t? ∈ rented
│ outcome! = alreadyRented
└──────────────────────────
```

Increasing or decreasing the stock level of a given title

The precondition exceptions and the schemas to handle them are as follows:

1. The title $t?$ is not in stock. This is handled by the *NotInStock* schema above.
2. The potential change would not leave a positive number of copies of the title in stock.

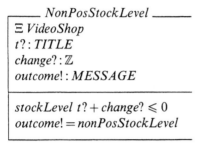

```
┌─── NonPosStockLevel ──────
│ Ξ VideoShop
│ t?: TITLE
│ change?: ℤ
│ outcome!: MESSAGE
├──────────────────────────
│ stockLevel t? + change? ⩽ 0
│ outcome! = nonPosStockLevel
└
```

3. The number of copies of the title in stock after the operation would be less than the number of copies out on rental.

```
┌─── TooManyRented ──────────────────
│ Ξ VideoShop
│ t?: TITLE
│ change?: ℤ
│ outcome!: MESSAGE
├────────────────────────────────────
│ stockLevel t? + change? < # rented ▷ {t?}
│ outcome! = tooManyRented
└
```

Removing a title from stock

The precondition exceptions and the schemas to handle them are as follows:

1. The title $t?$ is not in stock. This is handled by the *NotInStock* schema above.
2. There is at least one copy of the title out on rental.

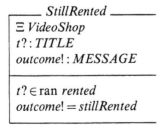

```
┌─── StillRented ──────
│ Ξ VideoShop
│ t?: TITLE
│ outcome!: MESSAGE
├──────────────────────
│ t? ∈ ran rented
│ outcome! = stillRented
└
```

Finding out the titles currently rented out by a given person

The precondition exception occurs when the person is not a member. This is handled by the *NotMember* schema above.

The number of copies of a given title currently out on rental

The precondition exception occurs when the title *t*? is not in stock. This is handled by the *NotInStock* schema above.

The number of copies of a given title currently in the shop

The precondition exception occurs when the title *t*? is not in stock. This is handled by the *NotInStock* schema above.

8.6 Total operation schemas

The total versions of the operation schemas are now defined using the above exception handling schemas.

$$TotalRentVideo \cong (RentVideo \land SuccessMessage)$$
$$\lor NotMember$$
$$\lor NotInStock$$
$$\lor AllCopiesOut$$
$$\lor AlreadyRented$$

$$TotalChangeStockLevel \cong (ChangeStockLevel \land SuccessMessage)$$
$$\lor NonPosStockLevel$$
$$\lor TooManyRented$$

$$TotalDeleteTitle \cong (DeleteTitle \land SuccessMessage)$$
$$\lor NotInStock$$
$$\lor StillRented$$

$$TotalTitlesOut \cong (TitlesOut \land SuccessMessage)$$
$$\lor NotMember$$

$$TotalCopiesRentedOut \cong (CopiesRentedOut \land SuccessMessage)$$
$$\lor NotInStock$$

$$TotalCopiesInShop \cong (CopiesInShop \land SuccessMessage)$$
$$\lor NotInStock$$

Exercises 8.1

1. Write schemas for operations to add and remove a member to or from the video shop.

2. Write a schema for the operation whereby a member returns a video to the shop.

3. How could you modify the state schema to allow a maximum of n videos to be rented by any given member?

4. Write a schema for an operation to output the set of all people who have a given title on rental.

5. Write a schema *SimilarTastes* to output the set of all people who have on rental at least one of the titles currently rented out to a given person.

6. Write exception handling schemas to totalise (make robust) the above operations.

7. Given the schema *AddTitle*, which adds a new title to the stock,

```
┌─────── AddTitle ──────────────────
│ Δ VideoShop
│ t? : TITLE
│ level? : ℕ₁
├────────────────────────────────────
│ stockLevel' = stockLevel ∪ {t? ↦ level?}
│ members' = members
│ rented' = rented
└────────────────────────────────────
```

what implicit precondition is present in this schema?

8. How could you modify the state schema *VideoShop* to allow any given member to rent more than one copy of a given title at the same time?

CHAPTER 9

Sequences

Aims

To introduce the concept of the sequence as a specialised sort of function, to introduce some sequence operators and to demonstrate the application of sequences in writing specifications.

Learning objectives

When you have completed this chapter, you should be able to:

- understand the kinds of system which may be modelled using sequences, and the styles of specification commonly used with sequences;
- understand the effect of relation, function and sequence operators when applied to sequences, and how to construct sequence-valued expressions using them;
- understand how the Z language may be extended by adding generic axiomatic definitions to specifications, and appreciate when it is appropriate to do so.

9.1 Introduction

Sequences embody the idea of the members of a set being arranged in a partic- ular *order*. Examples from everyday life are situations such as a supermarket checkout queue (a sequence of people), a phone directory (a sequence of names arranged alphabetically, each paired up with the corresponding phone number) or a queue at traffic lights (a sequence of vehicles).

Sequences allow us to model the common linear abstract data types of computer science, for example lists, stacks and queues. As artefacts in a speci- fication for a computer program, sequences may naturally be implemented in the target language as arrays, arrangements of pointers and records/structures, or object-oriented container classes. The translation for functional programming languages, where lists are built in and other recursive data types are easily defined, is even more straightforward.

9.2 Sequences in Z

A sequence is a restricted sort of function. The restriction is that the domain of a sequence must be a prefix subset of $\mathbb{N}_1$, the natural numbers excluding zero. In other words, if the sequence contains n maplets, its domain will be the set $1 .. n$. For example, given the type

[*PERSON*]   the set of all people

the function

$s : \mathbb{N}_1 \nrightarrow PERSON$ where $s = \{1 \mapsto tom, 2 \mapsto dick, 3 \mapsto harry\}$

is a sequence, whereas the function

$t : \mathbb{N}_1 \nrightarrow PERSON$ where $t = \{1 \mapsto tom, 2 \mapsto dick, 6 \mapsto harry\}$

is not a sequence.

We would refer to s as a *sequence of people*. In other words, a sequence defines an ordering of the items in its range. In the sequence s, *tom* is the first element, *dick* the second and *harry* the third. This sequence may be written using the shorthand notation

$s = \langle tom,\ dick,\ harry \rangle$

The *length* of a sequence is simply its cardinality, that is the number of pairs it contains. Thus the length of s is 3.

The *empty sequence* is represented by $\langle \rangle$. Its length is 0.

We would declare s as a sequence-valued variable as follows:

$s : \text{seq } PERSON$

This declaration is a shorthand for

$s : \mathbb{N} \nrightarrow PERSON$

together with the restriction

$\text{dom } s = 1 .. \#s$

This declaration allows s to be empty. To specify that s has at least one element, we can use the declaration

$s : \text{seq}_1\ PERSON$

In general, sequences may have repeated elements, for example

$\langle tom,\ dick,\ dick \rangle$

Clearly, a sequence with repeating elements is not injective (one-to-one), and vice versa. Therefore, to specify that, for a sequence t, repeating elements are not allowed, we may use the declaration for an *injective sequence*:

$t : \text{iseq}\ PERSON$

This is useful when we wish to model systems such as supermarket queues, where a person cannot be in two different places within a queue at the same time.

Here are some more examples of sequences:

$s = \langle \langle 1,2 \rangle,\ \langle 3,2,7 \rangle,\ \langle\ \rangle,\ \langle 1,6 \rangle \rangle$

is a sequence of sequences of integers, and would be declared as

$s : \text{seq}(\text{seq}\ \mathbb{Z})$ or perhaps $s : \text{iseq}(\text{iseq}\ \mathbb{Z})$

and

$t = \langle \{3,6\},\ \{\ \},\ \{6,8\},\ \{6,3\} \rangle$

is a sequence of sets of integers, and would be declared as

$t : \text{seq}(\mathbb{P}\ \mathbb{Z})$

and

$u = \langle \{5 \mapsto 6, 8 \mapsto 4\},\ \{2 \mapsto 10, 4 \mapsto 9\} \rangle$

is a sequence of homogeneous functions on the integers, and would be declared as

$u : \text{seq}(\mathbb{Z} \nrightarrow \mathbb{Z})$

Now, because a sequence is a restricted sort of function, which in turn is a restricted sort of relation, which is a restricted sort of set, we already have a rich collection of operators which can be used with sequences, provided the

Z type rules are not violated. However, the expressions resulting from applying such operators to sequences are not necessarily sequence-valued. For example, the expression

$$\{1, 2\} \lhd \{1 \mapsto tom, 2 \mapsto dick, 3 \mapsto harry\}$$

is the sequence

$$\{1 \mapsto tom, 2 \mapsto dick\}$$

whereas the expression

$$\{1, 3\} \lhd \{1 \mapsto tom, 2 \mapsto dick, 3 \mapsto harry\}$$

simplifies to

$$\{1 \mapsto tom, 3 \mapsto harry\}$$

which is a function but is not a sequence, because its domain is not a prefix subset of $\mathbb{N}_1$.

It is extremely important when writing specifications to be very clear about the types of the structures you are using, and the validity of expressions which you are associating with variables of those types in your predicates. Each declaration of a variable of a given type introduces implicit invariants into the schema in which it is used, and one of the most common sources of error in specifications is inconsistencies in the types of expressions. Software tools are available to help to identify these errors, but there is no substitute for clarity and depth of thought about the problem, and care in putting together your formal model of it. Here is another example.

The expression

$$\{1 \mapsto tom, 2 \mapsto dick, 3 \mapsto harry\} \cup \{1 \mapsto carol, 2 \mapsto janet\}$$

simplifies to

$$\{1 \mapsto tom, 1 \mapsto carol, 2 \mapsto dick, 2 \mapsto janet, 3 \mapsto harry\}$$

which is a relation that is neither a sequence nor a function. However, the expression

$$(\{1 \mapsto tom, 2 \mapsto dick, 3 \mapsto harry\} \cup \{1 \mapsto carol, 2 \mapsto janet\}) \rhd \{tom, dick\}$$

simplifies to

$$\{1 \mapsto carol, 2 \mapsto janet, 3 \mapsto harry\}$$

which is a sequence.

Exercises 9.1

1. Simplify and comment on the types of the following expressions:

   (i) $\langle a, b, c \rangle \cup \langle d, e, f \rangle$
   (ii) $\langle a, b, c \rangle \cup \langle a, b \rangle$
   (iii) $\langle a, b, c \rangle \cap \langle a, b \rangle$
   (iv) $\langle a, b, c \rangle \setminus \langle c \rangle$
   (v) $\langle a, b, c \rangle \rhd \{a, b\}$
   (vi) $\{1\} \lhd \langle a, b, c \rangle$
   (vii) $\langle a, b, c \rangle \oplus \langle d, e, f \rangle$
   (viii) $\langle a, b, c \rangle^{-1} \,;\langle d, e, f \rangle$
   (ix) $\langle 1, 2, 3 \rangle \rhd (\text{dom} \langle 1, 2, 3 \rangle)$

2. Given the sequence $s = \langle tom, dick, harry \rangle$, what is the value of the following?

   (i) $s\,1$ (s applied to 1)
   (ii) $s(\#s)$

3. Given the types

   $[PERSON]$ the set of all people
   $[CAR]$ the set of all cars

   write down possible values for the following variables and draw the corresponding pictures:
   (i) $p : \text{seq}(\mathbb{P}\,PERSON)$
   (ii) $q : \text{seq}(PERSON \nrightarrow CAR)$
   (iii) $r : \text{seq}(\text{seq}\,PERSON)$
   (iv) $s : \text{seq}((\mathbb{P}\,PERSON) \leftrightarrow CAR)$
   (v) $t : \mathbb{P}(\text{seq}\,CAR)$

9.3 Sequence operators

We will now introduce some additional operators for use with sequences.

The function *head* returns the first element in a non-empty sequence. For example,

$$head\langle tom, dick, harry \rangle = tom$$

Note that *head* returns *tom*, not the maplet $1 \mapsto tom$.

The function *tail* returns the sequence formed by removing the first maplet in a non-empty sequence (and, if necessary, modifying the domain of the result to make it a sequence). For example,

$$tail\langle tom, dick, harry \rangle = \langle dick, harry \rangle$$

The function *last* returns the last element in a non-empty sequence. For example,

$$last\langle tom, dick, harry \rangle = harry$$

Note that *last* returns *harry*, not the maplet $3 \mapsto harry$.

The function *front* returns the sequence formed by removing the last maplet in a non-empty sequence. For example,

$$front\langle tom, dick, harry \rangle = \langle tom, dick \rangle$$

The function *rev* returns the sequence formed by reversing the order of the elements in a given sequence. For example,

$$rev\langle tom, dick, harry \rangle = \langle harry, dick, tom \rangle$$

The *concatenation* operator $^\frown$ takes two sequences and returns the sequence formed by 'joining them together'. For example,

$$\langle tom, dick, harry \rangle ^\frown \langle andy, sandy, randy \rangle$$
$$= \langle tom, dick, harry, andy, sandy, randy \rangle$$

The *filter* operator $\upharpoonright$ takes a sequence and a set of the same type as the sequence's range set and returns the sequence formed by removing all maplets which do not contain, as their second element, members of the set. For example,

$$\langle tom, dick, harry \rangle \upharpoonright \{dick, harry, sandy\} = \langle dick, harry \rangle$$

The *squash* function takes any function f such that

$$\mathrm{dom}\, f \subseteq \mathbb{N}_1$$

and returns the sequence formed by modifying the domain of f, maintaining the original order which it defines. For example,

$$squash\{2 \mapsto dick, 3 \mapsto tom, 7 \mapsto harry\} = \{1 \mapsto dick, 2 \mapsto tom, 3 \mapsto harry\}$$

9.4 Generic constants

The above functions have been introduced informally, with English descriptions and examples. However, such functions may be formally defined as *generic constants*. They must be generic, because they must be able to operate on sequences of any given base type; that is, they must be capable of being applied to sequences of integers, sequences of people, sequences of sequences of integers, etc. For example, here is the definition from Spivey (1992) of sequence concatenation:

$$
\begin{array}{|l}
\hline\!\!\!\!=\!=\!=[X]\!=\!=\!=\\
\_ \frown \_ : \operatorname{seq} X \times \operatorname{seq} X \to \operatorname{seq} X \\
\hline
\forall s, t : \operatorname{seq} X \bullet \\
s \frown t = s \cup \{n : \operatorname{dom} t \bullet n + \#s \mapsto t(n)\} \\
\hline
\end{array}
$$

A generic constant has one or more generic formal parameters. In the above example, the formal parameter is X, which stands for any actual parameter set supplied implicitly when the $\frown$ operator is used. The declaration

$$\_ \frown \_ : \operatorname{seq} X \times \operatorname{seq} X \to \operatorname{seq} X$$

states that $\frown$ is an infix function (indicated by the position of the underscores which shows where the parameters should go) which may be applied to any pair of sequences of the same type, to return another sequence of that type. There is a notation for explicitly supplying actual generic parameters when the operator is used, but this may be left implicit. For example, in the expression

$$\langle 1, 2, 3 \rangle \frown \langle 4, 5 \rangle$$

the formal parameter X has clearly been instantiated as $\mathbb{Z}$. The predicate

$$\forall s, t : \operatorname{seq} X \bullet s \frown t = s \cup \{n : \operatorname{dom} t \bullet n + \#s \mapsto t(n)\}$$

defines the sequence returned by the operator to consist of the pairs from the first operand, together with the pairs from the second one after making an appropriate shift to its domain.

As a further example, here is a generic constant definition for the *head* function:

$$
\begin{array}{|l}
\hline\!\!\!\!=\!=\!=[X]\!=\!=\!=\\
head : \operatorname{seq}_1 X \to X \\
\hline
\forall s : \operatorname{seq}_1 X \bullet head\ s = s\ 1 \\
\hline
\end{array}
$$

The declaration states that *head* is a prefix function (no underscores) which may be applied to any non-empty sequence to return the first element of that sequence. The predicate states that the element returned by *head* is precisely that which would result from applying the sequence to the number 1. The type seq_1 is required because *head* is not defined for the empty sequence. It is also a requirement when defining generic constants that the definition must uniquely determine the value of the constant for all possible values of the formal parameters.

Similar generic constant definitions are used to define many other standard Z operators, and we can use them to define new operators for our own specifications. However, this should not be done to excess. New operators should only be introduced if they improve the clarity of the specification. Examples would be if the operator was required in several places in the specification, or if the expressions required as an alternative to the operator were very complex and opaque. It should be mentioned that it is also possible to define generic *schemas* in Z; see Spivey (1992) for further details.

Exercises 9.2

1. Simplify the following expressions:

    (i) $\langle 1, 2, 3 \rangle \frown \langle \rangle$

    (ii) $\mathrm{dom}\langle a, b, c \rangle$

    (iii) $\mathrm{ran}\langle 1, 1, 2 \rangle$

    (iv) $\{a \mapsto 2, b \mapsto 3, c \mapsto 1\}^{-1}$

    (v) $\mathrm{dom}(\langle 1, 2 \rangle \frown \langle 3, 4 \rangle)$

    (vi) $\{1\} \lhd tail(\langle a, b, c \rangle)$

    (vii) $\mathrm{dom}((front\langle 1, 3, 5, 7 \rangle)^{-1})$

    (viii) $head(tail(tail(\langle 1, 7, 9, 2, 2 \rangle \frown \langle 2, 4, 5 \rangle)))$

    (ix) $last(tail \ (\langle \langle \rangle, \langle 1 \rangle \ \langle 1, 2 \rangle, \langle 1, 2, 3 \rangle, \langle 1, 2, 3, 4 \rangle \rangle)) \frown \langle 1, 2 \rangle$

    (x) $squash(3 .. 5 \lhd \langle a, b, c, d, e, f \rangle)$

    (xi) $rev(\langle 2, 3, 4, 6, 8 \rangle \upharpoonright (\mathrm{dom}\langle a, b, c \rangle))$

2. Given the declaration *s*: iseq $\mathbb{Z}$, write a predicate to specify that the numbers in the range of *s* are in non-descending order.

3. Give a generic constant definition for the function *tail*.

4. Give a generic constant definition for the function *for* which returns the prefix subsequence of a given sequence from its beginning up to a given position. If the given position is greater than or equal to the length of the sequence, the operation should return the whole sequence. For example,

    $\langle tom, dick, harry \rangle \ for \ 2 = \langle tom, dick \rangle$
    $\langle tom, dick, harry \rangle \ for \ 7 = \langle tom, dick, harry \rangle$

9.5 disjoint, partition

We can specify that a sequence of sets

$$\langle A_1, A_2, \ldots, A_n \rangle$$

is *pairwise disjoint*, that is none of the sets intersect with each other, using the expression

disjoint$\langle A_1, A_2, \ldots, A_n \rangle$

For example, the following is true

disjoint$\langle \{1, 2, 3\}, \{7, 8\}, \{12, 13, 6\} \rangle$

A sequence of sets

$$\langle A_1, A_2, \ldots, A_n \rangle$$

partitions a set S iff the union of all the sets in the sequence is S, and the sets in the sequence are pairwise disjoint. This is captured by the expression

$\langle A_1, A_2, \ldots, A_n \rangle$ partition S

For example, the following is true

$\langle \{1, 2\}, \{3, 4\}, \{5\} \rangle$ partition $\{1, 2, 3, 4, 5\}$

We will use this concept in the next section.

9.6 The university badminton club revisited

This specification was introduced in Chapters 4 and 5. We will now refine part of it to describe the activity in the hall, which contains one badminton court, where members of the club come to play. People in the hall are either playing a game on the court, or effectively in a queue, waiting to play. We will model this queue as an injective sequence called *waiting*, and represent those playing a game by the set *onCourt*. The specification could be implemented as a computer program to run on a portable machine kept by the club secretary, or more likely, as a system of paper records of club membership, together with a wooden name board to indicate who is queuing and who is playing a game.

Recall that the state in the original example was described by the schema

```
┌─────── ClubState ────────
│ badminton : ℙ STUDENT
│ hall : ℙ STUDENT
├──────────────────────────
│ hall ⊆ badminton
│ # hall ≤ maxPlayers
└──────────────────────────
```

We will reuse and extend this description, by including it in a new state schema, *ClubState2*:

```
┌───── ClubState2 ──────────────────
│ ClubState
│ onCourt : ℙ STUDENT
│ waiting : iseq STUDENT
├────────────────────────────────────
│ ⟨onCourt, ran waiting⟩ partition hall
└────────────────────────────────────
```

The predicate

$$\langle onCourt, \text{ran } waiting \rangle \text{ partition } hall$$

states that everyone in the hall is either playing a game or waiting to do so, and that nobody is both waiting and playing at the same time!

The initial state, as before, is a club with no members:

```
┌── InitClubState2 ───
│ ClubState2'
├─────────────────────
│ badminton' = { }
└─────────────────────
```

Note that if *badminton'* is empty, the state invariant implies that all of the sets in the state are empty. We will now specify three operations.

Beginning a new game

For a new game to begin, there must not be a game currently in progress

$$onCourt = \varnothing$$

and there must be at least two people in the queue (one cannot play badminton by oneself!)

$$\# waiting \geq 2$$

If there are four or more people in the queue, then four people will play in the new game.

$$\# \ waiting \geqslant 4 \Rightarrow \# \ onCourt' = 4$$

If there are less than four people in the hall, then either two people or three people will play in the new game.

$$\# \ waiting < 4 \Rightarrow (\# \ onCourt' = 2) \vee (\# \ onCourt' = 3)$$

The rules of the club state that the people to play the next game will comprise the person at the front of the queue

$$head \ waiting \in onCourt'$$

together with the appropriate number of people as defined above, selected by him/her from up to the next five positions in the queue

$$onCourt' \subseteq ran(1 .. 6 \lhd waiting)$$

Note that this predicate is non-deterministic in that it simply states that all the people in the new game must have come from the first six places in the queue. We can specify the rules for choosing the players, but our Z specification cannot capture the vindictiveness and favouritism involved in making the decision!

Finally, the predicate

$$waiting' = waiting \restriction ((ran \ waiting) \setminus onCourt')$$

states that the new queue is equal to the old queue with those chosen for the game removed. We subtract the players chosen for the new game from the range of *waiting*, and then filter the sequence with this set.

The operation schema is as follows:

```
┌──── NewGame ─────────────────────
│ Δ ClubState2
├───────────────────────────────────
│ onCourt = ∅
│ # waiting ⩾ 2
│ # waiting ⩾ 4 ⇒ # onCourt' = 4
│ # waiting < 4 ⇒ (# onCourt' = 2) ∨ (# onCourt' = 3)
│ head waiting ∈ onCourt'
│ onCourt' ⊆ ran(1 .. 6 ◁ waiting)
│ waiting' = waiting ↾ ((ran waiting) \ onCourt')
│ hall' = hall
│ badminton' = badminton
└───────────────────────────────────
```

Ending a game

To end a game, there must be one taking place!

$$onCourt \neq \{\}$$

The players come off the court

$$onCourt' = \{\}$$

and join the back of the queue in an unspecified order.

$$\exists s : \text{iseq } STUDENT \bullet (\text{ran } s = onCourt \wedge waiting' = waiting \frown s)$$

Again, this predicate is non-deterministic in that it describes the relationship required between the sets without actually stating how the operation is to achieve this. This may seem a little strange to those used to writing programs, where one must state specifically how a task is to be done, but at the specification level we are free to think at a higher level of abstraction: to write an expression which characterises the relationship between a 'before' state and an 'after' state, without necessarily indicating how this is to be achieved. The specification task is not about writing recipes for achieving results, but simply stating what those results should be. (Some clubs have a policy that the winners of the game get to go ahead of the losers in the waiting list, but in a doubles game, there is still uncertainty about which of the winners and which of the losers goes ahead of the other!)

The operation schema is as follows:

```
┌─── FinishGame ──────────────────
│ Δ ClubState2
├─────────────────────────────────
│ onCourt ≠ {}
│ onCourt' = {}
│ ∃s : iseq STUDENT •
│ (ran s = onCourt ∧ waiting' = waiting ⌢ s)
│ hall' = hall
│ badminton' = badminton
└─────────────────────────────────
```

A person leaving the hall

We assume that our person p? does not leave in the middle of a game!

$$p? \in \text{ran } waiting$$

We use $\rhd$ to remove our person from the queue, and *squash* to restore the result to be a valid sequence.

$$waiting' = squash(waiting \rhd \{p?\})$$

The person is removed from the hall by the predicate

$$hall' = hall \setminus \{p?\}$$

The operation schema is as follows:

─────── *LeaveHall* ───────
Δ *ClubState2*
$p? : STUDENT$

───────────────────────
$p? \in \text{ran } waiting$
$waiting' = squash(waiting \rhd \{p?\})$
$hall' = hall \setminus \{p?\}$
$badminton' = badminton$

Note that we have not explicitly stated that *onCourt* is not changed. This is implicitly specified by the state invariant. However, it is sometimes considered to be good practice, in the interests of clarity, to make such properties explicit in the operation schema.

This is a new version of the *LeaveHall* schema, which was first written for the simplified system state described in Chapters 4 and 5. We could have reused and modified the original version, but this would not have improved the readability of the specification. To complete the specification, we would have to modify the other operation schemas from Chapters 4 and 5 to operate on the new state, and we would have to totalise all operations using the schema calculus. You may wish to try this as an additional exercise.

───

Exercises 9.3

1. Write a schema to specify an operation for a person to enter the hall and join the back of the *waiting* queue.
2. Write a Z predicate which states that a given sequence of characters s is a substring of a given sequence of characters t.
3. Write a Z expression for the number of occurrences of a natural number n in a sequence of natural numbers s.

4. What characteristics must a sequence possess if its inverse is also a sequence?

5. Write a Z predicate which states that a given sequence of characters s is a palindrome; that is, it spells the same backwards as it does forwards.

A third specification: Project allocation

10.1 Introduction

In the previous chapter, we developed a specification which used a sequence to model a queue of people. In this chapter, we will take this a stage further by using sequences in combination with functions to model a more complex situation, namely the allocation of undergraduate projects on a university degree course.

10.2 Allocation of undergraduate projects: the problem

A university requires a computerised system to manage the allocation of the individual projects undertaken by its final-year degree students. Each student must be allocated to a personal supervisor from the lecturing staff. Each lecturer has a maximum number of students which s/he is required to supervise. Each student and each lecturer must list their areas of interest (in descending order of their enthusiasm for the topic!) and the system must attempt to allocate students to supervisors in such a way that the maximum contentedness with the result is created. Contentedness is a difficult concept; we all have an intuitive idea of how much of it we possess at any given time, but it is not easy to quantify in the context of a potentially large group of students and lecturers. Inevitably, some people will be more content with the allocation than others! To make things worse, we are trying to specify contentedness in a formal language, where we must give a precise definition. This means that we have to simplify and make compromises. We will arbitrarily decide that the priority is to allocate the student currently under consideration his/her most desired choice of topic from those which are available (i.e. those which are on the 'areas of interest' list of at least one lecturer who has not already got a full complement of students to supervise), the student being allocated to the lecturer who has this topic highest on his/her list of preferences. If more than one lecturer has the topic at the same level of priority, an arbitrary choice of supervisor can be made from these lecturers. We are thus putting the students' wishes above those of the lecturers.

10.3 Basic types and the system state schema

These are

$[PERSON]$ the set of all people
$[TOPIC]$ the set of all academic areas of interest

```
┌─── ProjectAlloc ──────────────────────────────
│ studInterests, lecInterests : PERSON ⇸ iseq TOPIC
│ allocation : PERSON ⇸ PERSON
│ maxPlaces : PERSON ⇸ ℕ
├──────────────────────────────────────────────
│ dom studInterests ∩ dom lecInterests = { }
│ dom allocation ⊆ dom studInterests
│ ran allocation ⊆ dom lecInterests
│ dom maxPlaces = dom lecInterests
│ ∀lec : dom maxPlaces
│     • #(allocation ▷ {lec}) ⩽ maxPlaces lec
└──────────────────────────────────────────────
```

The functions *studInterests* and *lecInterests* map individual students and lecturers respectively to their preference lists. The lists are represented by injective sequences of topics, which means that a given topic cannot appear in a given list more than once; that is, there are no duplicates. The lists are assumed to be sorted into descending order of preference for the topics.

The set of all students in the system is

dom *studInterests*

and the set of all lecturers in the system is

dom *lecInterests*

The function *allocation* relates the students who have been allocated a project to their supervisors. It is a function because this means that any given student can be related to at most one supervisor.

The function *maxPlaces* relates each lecturer to the maximum number of students which they are required to supervise. This specification will not allow any lecturer to supervise more than their maximum number of students. We allow the possibility that a lecturer may be in the system with *no* places as his/her maximum, so that the system may contain the information as to the lecturer's interests for some future allocation.

The predicate

dom *studInterests* $\cap$ dom *lecInterests* $= \{\,\}$

specifies that a person in the system cannot be both a student and a supervisor.

The predicates

dom *allocation* $\subseteq$ dom *studInterests*
ran *allocation* $\subseteq$ dom *lecInterests*

specify that those students and lecturers who have been allocated to projects must be students and lecturers in the system.

The predicate

dom *maxPlaces* $=$ dom *lecInterests*

specifies that *all* lecturers in the system have a designated maximum number of supervisions which they may undertake.

The initial state is as follows:

```
┌─ InitProjectAlloc ────
│ ProjectAlloc'
├───────────────────────
│ lecInterests' = {}
│ studInterests' = {}
└───────────────────────
```

These values for *lecInterests'* and *studInterests'* imply that all of the sets in the abstract state are empty, and all of the state invariant predicates are satisfied, so that this is a valid state for the system.

10.4 Operations

We will now specify the successful cases of operations to add a student to the system, add a lecturer to the system, allocate a supervisor to a student, deallocate a supervisor from a student, remove a topic from a lecturer's preference list and output the set of all lecturers available for the supervision of a given topic.

Adding a student to the system

The inputs required for this operation are a student and that student's list of preferences for his/her project topic. The list is assumed to be organised in descending order of the student's preference for the topics therein.

```
┌──────── AddStudent ───────────────────────
│ Δ ProjectAlloc
│ s? : PERSON
│ ts? : iseq TOPIC
├───────────────────────────────────────────
│ s? ∉ dom studInterests ∪ dom lecInterests
│ studInterests' = studInterests ∪ {s? ↦ ts?}
│ lecInterests' = lecInterests
│ allocation' = allocation
│ maxPlaces' = maxPlaces
└───────────────────────────────────────────
```

The student must not already be in the system, as either a lecturer or a student!

$$s? \notin \text{dom } studInterests \cup \text{dom } lecInterests$$

The appropriate maplet is added to the *studInterests* function.

$$studInterests' = studInterests \cup \{s? \mapsto ts?\}$$

Note that it would be sufficient to have the precondition

$$s? \notin \text{dom } studInterests$$

because

$$s? \notin \text{dom } lecInterests$$

is implied by the postcondition

$$studInterests' = studInterests \cup \{s? \mapsto ts?\}$$

and the 'after' state invariant

$$\mathrm{dom}\ studInterests' \cap \mathrm{dom}\ lecInterests' = \{\ \}$$

In fact, we don't need an explicit precondition at all, as the above postcondition implies that either

$$s? \mapsto ts? \in studInterests$$

in which case the operation has no effect on the state, or

$$s? \notin \mathrm{dom}\ studInterests$$

This is because *studInterests* is a function, so *s?* cannot be mapped to more than one range element. However, in an implementation of the system, we would like the system to produce a message to tell the user when such events occur, so we will leave the explicit precondition in the schema, and write appropriate error case schemas to produce a total version of the operation.

Adding a lecturer to the system

The inputs required for this operation are a lecturer, the list of topics which that lecturer is prepared to supervise and the maximum number of students which the lecturer may supervise. Again, the list of topics is assumed to be organised in descending order of the lecturer's preference for the topics.

┌───── *AddLecturer* ──────────────────
│ $\Delta\ ProjectAlloc$
│ $l? : PERSON$
│ $ts? : \mathrm{iseq}\ TOPIC$
│ $maxAlloc? : \mathbb{N}_1$
├──────────────────────────────
│ $l? \notin \mathrm{dom}\ studInterests \cup \mathrm{dom}\ lecInterests$
│ $lecInterests' = lecInterests \cup \{l? \mapsto ts?\}$
│ $maxPlaces' = maxPlaces \cup \{l? \mapsto maxAlloc?\}$
│ $studInterests' = studInterests$
│ $allocation' = allocation$
└──────────────────────────────

The lecturer must not already be in the system, as either a lecturer or a student!

$$l? \notin \text{dom } studInterests \cup \text{dom } lecInterests$$

The appropriate maplet is added to the *lecInterests* function

$$lecInterests' = lecInterests \cup \{l? \mapsto ts?\}$$

and to the *maxPlaces* function.

$$maxPlaces' = maxPlaces \cup \{l? \mapsto maxAlloc?\}$$

Exercises 10.1

1. Write a predicate which specifies a state where there are no unallocated students.
2. Write a predicate which specifies a state where all students in the system are unallocated.
3. Write a schema for an operation to remove a student from the system.
4. Write a schema for an operation to remove a lecturer from the system.
5. Write a Z expression for the set of all the students allocated to a given supervisor *s*.
6. Write a Z expression for the set of all students with the same supervisor as a given student *p*.

Allocating a student to a supervisor

The input to this operation is the student to be allocated. The operation must allocate this student to a supervisor in such a way that the student gets to do the highest priority topic from his/her list for which a supervisor is available. ('Available' means that the topic appears in the preference list of at least one supervisor who still has places left for supervisions.) Remember that preference lists are assumed to be sorted into descending order of preference. Additionally, the student is to be allocated to the lecturer who has this topic highest on his/her list of preferences. If more than one lecturer has the topic at the same level of priority, an arbitrary choice of supervisor will be made from these lecturers.

```
┌─────── Allocate ──────────────────────────────────────────
│ Δ ProjectAlloc
│ s? : PERSON
├────────────────────────────────────────────────────────────
│ s? ∈ dom studInterests
│ s? ∉ dom allocation
│
│ ∃ sup : dom lecInterests; t : TOPIC; i, j : ℕ
│  | maxPlaces sup > # (allocation ▷ {sup})
│    ∧ i ↦ t ∈ studInterests s?
│    ∧ j ↦ t ∈ lecInterests sup
│  • (
│      ∀ lec : dom lecInterests; k : ℕ | maxPlaces lec > # (allocation ▷ {lec})
│        • (
│            (k ↦ t ∈ lecInterests lec ⇒ k ⩾ j )
│            ∧
│            (ran(1 .. i − 1 ◁ studInterests s?) ∩ ran(lecInterests lec) = { })
│          )
│      ∧ allocation' = allocation ∪ {s? ↦ sup}
│    )
│ studInterests' = studInterests
│ lecInterests' = lecInterests
└────────────────────────────────────────────────────────────
```

The student must be in the system, and must not be already allocated to a supervisor.

$$s? \in \text{dom } studInterests$$
$$s? \notin \text{dom } allocation$$

The other preconditions and postconditions of interest are specified by the rather complex quantified expression above, which we will look at piece by piece.

There is a supervisor who has places left for project supervision and who has one of the students' topics on his/her list of preferences:

$$\exists \, sup : \text{dom } lecInterests; \; t : TOPIC; \; i, j : \mathbb{N}$$
$$| \, maxPlaces \, sup > \# \, (allocation \rhd \{sup\})$$
$$\wedge \, i \mapsto t \in studInterests \, s?$$
$$\wedge \, j \mapsto t \in lecInterests \, sup$$

There are no supervisors available who have this topic at a higher priority in their list of preferences than the given supervisor

$$\forall \, lec : \text{dom } lecInterests; \; k : \mathbb{N} \, | \, maxPlaces \, lec > \# \, (allocation \rhd \{lec\})$$
$$\bullet \, ($$
$$\quad (k \mapsto t \in lecInterests \, lec \Rightarrow k \geqslant j \,)$$

and there are no supervisors available who are interested in any of the topics which the student has at a higher priority than the given topic.

$$\land$$
$$(\mathrm{ran}(1 \mathinner{\ldotp\ldotp} i - 1 \lhd \mathit{studInterests}\ s?) \cap \mathrm{ran}(\mathit{lecInterests}\ \mathit{lec}) = \{\,\})$$
$$)$$

The allocation of the student to the supervisor is specified by

$$\mathit{allocation'} = \mathit{allocation} \cup \{s? \mapsto \mathit{sup}\}$$

Deallocating a student from a supervisor

The input to this operation is the student to be deallocated. The precondition is that the student is allocated to a supervisor.

```
┌─────── DeAllocate ──────────────────
│ Δ ProjectAlloc
│ s? : PERSON
├──────────────────────────────────────
│ ∃ sup : dom lecInterests
│   • (s? ↦ sup ∈ allocation
│      ∧ allocation' = allocation \ {s? ↦ sup})
│ studInterests' = studInterests
│ lecInterests' = lecInterests
│
└──────────────────────────────────────
```

Allocation policies

We now have operations to add new people to the system and to allocate students to supervisors according to the preferences of both. However, we have said nothing about the temporal aspects of our allocation policy. The initial state is one with no people in the system. Clearly we must first use our 'add' operations to place some people into the system, before we can allocate any students to supervisors. In a real system, we might add all the lecturers who are designated for project supervision first, and then either add each student in turn in the order in which they show up for registration, immediately allocating each student to a supervisor (first-come, first-served policy), or add all the students, and then randomly allocate them to supervisors until there are no unallocated students left in the system. A more sophisticated policy could be specified in an effort to improve the overall 'contentedness' with the allocation; that is, a policy which pleases most of the people most of the time, rather than the first students to come along getting their highest preferences, and later students getting whatever is still available. In the interests of simplicity, we will leave such considerations out of the current specification, but you may wish to think about how such ideas could be represented in Z. Of course, real life is never straightforward, and it is possible that all supervisors will have used up their allocation while there are still students unallocated, so that extra supervisors have to be added, or that there are students whose chosen preferences for topics do not occur in the preference lists for any supervisors, in which case further compromises will be necessary.

Removing a topic from a lecturer's preference list

The lecturer must be in the system and the topic must be in the lecturer's preference list. If the lecturer is already allocated to supervise this topic, it's too bad – the lecturer has made an agreement! However, the lecturer will not have to take on any further students for this topic.

$$
\begin{array}{|l}
\underline{\quad RemoveLecsTopic\ }\underline{}\\
\Delta\ ProjectAlloc\\
l?:PERSON\\
t?:TOPIC\\
\hline
l? \in \mathrm{dom}\ lecInterests\\
t? \in \mathrm{ran}(lecInterests\ l?)\\
lecInterests' = lecInterests \oplus \{l? \mapsto squash(lecInterests\ l? \rhd \{t?\})\}\\
maxPlaces' = maxPlaces\\
studInterests' = studInterests\\
allocation' = allocation\\
\end{array}
$$

Range anti-restriction is used to remove the topic from the sequence, and *squash* is used to make the result into a sequence. An alternative would have been to use an existentially quantified expression as follows:

$$
\begin{aligned}
&\exists\ higher,\ lower: \mathrm{iseq}\ TOPIC\\
&\quad \bullet\ (lecInterests\ l? = higher \frown \langle t? \rangle \frown lower\\
&\qquad \wedge\ lecInterests'\ l? = higher \frown lower)
\end{aligned}
$$

The set of all lecturers available for supervision of a given topic

For a given lecturer to be a member of this set, the topic must be in that lecturer's list of preferences and the lecturer must still have supervision places available.

```
┌─── LecsAvailable ──────────────────────────────
│ Ξ ProjectAlloc
│ t? : TOPIC
│ ps! : ℙ PERSON
├──────────────────────────────────────────────
│ ps! = { p : dom lecInterests | t? ∈ ran(lecInterests p)
│               ∧ maxPlaces p > # (allocation ▷ {p})}
└──────────────────────────────────────────────
```

Exercises 10.2

1. Write a schema for an operation to add a new topic to a lecturer's priority list at a given position. If the position is greater than the length of the list, the topic should be added to the back of the list.
2. Write a Z expression for the set of all students who are doing project topic t.
3. Write a schema for an operation to output the topic which a given student was allocated for his/her project.
4. Write a Z expression for the set of all unallocated students for whom none of their chosen topics are available for supervision.
5. Write a Z expression for the set of all students who were allocated their nth choice of topic in order of preference, where n is a natural number (excluding zero).

10.5 Error handling schemas

The following free type represents the set of output messages required to construct total versions of the above operations, and for reports from the query operations which are defined below:

$MESSAGE ::= success \mid isStudent \mid isLecturer \mid notStudent \mid isAllocated$
$\qquad \mid noLecAvailable \mid notAllocated \mid notLecturer \mid notListedTopic$

The *success* message is used to indicate that an operation has been successfully completed, using the following schema:

$SuccessMessage \triangleq [outcome! : MESSAGE \mid outcome! = success]$

The precondition for the *AddStudent* operation is

$s? \notin dom\ studInterests \cup dom\ lecInterests$

The exceptions to this operation occur if $s?$ is already a student or a lecturer.

In these cases, the state does not change and the appropriate message is produced. This is specified by the following schemas:

```
┌─── IsStudent ────────
│ Ξ ProjectAlloc
│ s? : PERSON
│ outcome! : MESSAGE
├──────────────────────
│ s? ∈ dom studInterests
│ outcome! = isStudent
│
└──────────────────────
```

```
┌─── IsLecturer ────────
│ Ξ ProjectAlloc
│ s? : PERSON
│ outcome! : MESSAGE
├──────────────────────
│ s? ∈ dom lecInterests
│ outcome! = isLecturer
│
└──────────────────────
```

For the *AddLecturer* operation, the exceptions are specified by the same schemas with appropriate renaming:

IsStudent [$s?/l?$]
IsLecturer [$s?/l?$]

The preconditions for the *Allocate* operation are that the student is in the system and is not already allocated:

$s? \in$ dom *studInterests*
$s? \notin$ dom *allocation*

and that there is at least one lecturer with places left who has at least one of the student's preferred topics on his/her preference list:

$\exists sup :$ dom *lecInterests* •
    maxPlaces sup $> \#$ (*allocation* $\triangleright$ {*sup*})
    $\land$ ran(*studInterests s?*) $\cap$ ran(*lecInterests sup*) $\neq$ { }

This leads to the following exception schemas:

```
┌─── NotStudent ──────
│ Ξ ProjectAlloc
│ s? : PERSON
│ outcome! : MESSAGE
├──────────────────────
│ s? ∉ dom studInterests
│ outcome! = notStudent
└──────────────────────
```

```
┌─── IsAllocated ──────
│ Ξ ProjectAlloc
│ s? : PERSON
│ outcome! : MESSAGE
├──────────────────────
│ s? ∈ dom allocation
│ outcome! = isAllocated
└──────────────────────
```

```
┌───── NoLecAvailable ──────────────────────────
│ Ξ ProjectAlloc
│ s? : PERSON
│ outcome! : MESSAGE
├────────────────────────────────────────────────
│ ¬ ∃ sup : dom lecInterests •
│     maxPlaces sup > # (allocation ▷ {sup})
│     ∧ ran(studInterests s?) ∩ ran(lecInterests sup) ≠ { }
│ outcome! = noLecAvailable
└────────────────────────────────────────────────
```

The precondition for the *DeAllocate* operation is that the student is allocated to a supervisor. This leads to the following exception schema:

```
┌───── NotAllocated ──────
│ Ξ ProjectAlloc
│ s? : PERSON
│ outcome! : MESSAGE
├──────────────────────────
│ s? ∉ dom allocation
│ outcome! = notAllocated
└──────────────────────────
```

The preconditions for the *RemoveLecsTopic* schema are that the person is a lecturer in the system and that the topic is in the lecturer's preference list.

$l? \in$ dom *lecInterests*
$t? \in$ ran(*lecInterests l?*)

This leads to the following exception schemas:

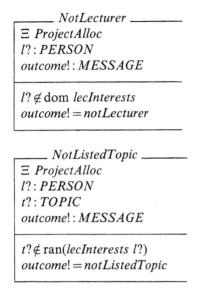

NotLecturer
Ξ ProjectAlloc
l? : PERSON
outcome! : MESSAGE

l? ∉ dom lecInterests
outcome! = notLecturer

NotListedTopic
Ξ ProjectAlloc
l? : PERSON
t? : TOPIC
outcome! : MESSAGE

t? ∉ ran(lecInterests l?)
outcome! = notListedTopic

10.6 Total operations

We can now define the total versions of the operation schemas using the above exception handling schemas.

$TotalAddStudent \;\hat{=}\; (AddStudent \land SuccessMessage)$
$\qquad\qquad \lor\; IsStudent$
$\qquad\qquad \lor\; IsLecturer$

$TotalAddLecturer \;\hat{=}\; (AddLecturer \land SuccessMessage)$
$\qquad\qquad \lor\; IsStudent\;[s?\,/\,l?]$
$\qquad\qquad \lor\; IsLecturer\;[s?\,/\,l?]$

$TotalAllocate \;\hat{=}\; (Allocate \land SuccessMessage)$
$\qquad\qquad \lor\; NotStudent$
$\qquad\qquad \lor\; IsAllocated$
$\qquad\qquad \lor\; NoLecAvailable$

$TotalDeAllocate \;\hat{=}\; (DeAllocate \land SuccessMessage)$
$\qquad\qquad \lor\; NotAllocated$

$TotalRemoveLecsTopic \;\hat{=}\; (RemoveLecsTopic \land SuccessMessage)$
$\qquad\qquad \lor\; NotLecturer$
$\qquad\qquad \lor\; NotListedTopic$

The LecsAvailable operation has no precondition; it may be applied in any state.

10.7 A new concept: operation schema composition

The composition of two operation schemas A and B is a schema which specifies the effect of doing operation A followed by operation B. It is written $A \,; B$.

Let A and B be the following schemas:

```
┌─ A ──────────┐     ┌─ B ──────────────┐
│ a, a', c! : ℤ │     │ a, a', b? : ℤ     │
├──────────────┤     ├──────────────────┤
│ a' = a + 42   │     │ b? < 10           │
│ c! = a'       │     │ a' = a + b?       │
└──────────────┘     └──────────────────┘
```

All variables with the same name (ignoring decorations) in the two schemas must also have the same type. The composition is formed as follows.

Firstly, we rename each variable which is both an 'after' variable (primed) in A and a 'before' variable (unprimed) in B to the same, new name. (See Chapter 4 if you need a reminder of what is meant by renaming.) In our example, we will rename a' from A and a from B to the new name a_c to give the schemas $NewA \,\widehat{=}\, A[a_c/a']$ and $NewB \,\widehat{=}\, B[a_c/a]$:

```
┌─ NewA ──────────┐     ┌─ NewB ──────────────┐
│ a, a_c, c! : ℤ   │     │ a_c, a', b? : ℤ       │
├─────────────────┤     ├──────────────────────┤
│ a_c = a + 42     │     │ b? < 10               │
│ c! = a_c         │     │ a' = a_c + b?         │
└─────────────────┘     └──────────────────────┘
```

Next, we conjoin the two schemas, and hide the renamed variables. (Again, see Chapter 4 if you need a reminder of what is meant by hiding.) In our example, this gives the schema

$$AcompB \,\widehat{=}\, A \,; B$$

where

$$AcompB \,\widehat{=}\, (A[a_c/a'] \land B[a_c/a]) \setminus (a_c)$$

```
┌─ AcompB ───────────┐
│ a, a', b?, c! : ℤ   │
├────────────────────┤
│ ∃a_c : ℤ            │
│ • (a_c = a + 42     │
│    ∧ c! = a_c       │
│    ∧ b? < 10        │
│    ∧ a' = a_c + b?) │
└────────────────────┘
```

10.8 Changing supervisor

We will now use the concept of schema composition to define an operation whereby a student, already assigned to a supervisor, changes to another supervisor. This operation may be specified as the composition of the *DeAllocate* and *Allocate* operations. However, this would allow the possibility that the new supervisor was the same as the old supervisor. We can disallow this by conjoining the result with a schema which specifies that the 'before' supervisor and the 'after' supervisor are different.

```
┌─── SupsDiffer ──────────
│ Δ ProjectAlloc
│ s? : PERSON
├────────────────────────
│ ∃ old, new : dom lecInterests
│   • (s? ↦ old ∈ allocation ∧
│      s? ↦ new ∈ allocation' ∧
│      old ≠ new)
└────────────────────────
```

The operation to change supervisor may now be specified.

$ChangeSup \cong (DeAllocate \, ; Allocate) \land SupsDiffer$

Note that the *Allocate* schema is non-deterministic in that more than one final state is possible (more than one lecturer may have places left and have the appropriate topic at the same priority on their list). Thus the *ChangeSup* operation is also non-deterministic. If we were to compose such a schema with a schema for which not all of those final states satisfied the precondition, then only the valid final states would count in the composition schema.

Exercise 10.3

How could we specify allocation which was on a first-come, first-served basis?

10.9 Abstraction

This specification is a little more abstract than the video shop specification of Chapter 8. In the latter, we used a *number* to represent the stock level of each video, comparing this number with the number of copies of the video out on rental when deciding whether any copies were available for rental. Modelling the concept of the whereabouts of copies using numbers is an example of modelling at a *low* level of abstraction, akin to modelling an algorithm in a programming language. (See the answer to question 8 of Exercises 8.1 for a suggested alternative, more abstract, representation for the concept of a video copy for this specification.) This type of modelling may lead to a specification which is easier to implement in a programming language, but may also lead to a lack of clarity in the specification, and possibly less flexibility if it later becomes necessary to modify the specification to accommodate new requirements.

In contrast, the project allocation specification has a higher level of abstraction, with some use of non-determinism as already discussed. It may not be quite so obvious how to produce an implementation from such a specification, as it very much specifies *what* the system must do and not *how* it is to do it. However, the greater level of abstraction means that we can study the problem in its own right without having to be concerned about the paraphernalia of how we are eventually going to produce a program. So is it better to write specifications with a low level of abstraction, or a high level of abstraction? As always in the field of science, the answer is 'it depends'! The important thing is that the specification correctly represents the requirements, and is clear and understandable to all those who must read, discuss and use it. There are techniques in Z for writing specifications at a high level of abstraction, and then refining them to a lower level of abstraction, while proving that the properties of the original specification are preserved, thus getting the best of both worlds. However, these techniques are beyond the scope of this book.

CHAPTER 11

Two outline Z specifications

Aims

To apply the preceding material to some more demanding specifications, and to illustrate the use of generic constants.

Learning objectives

When you have completed this chapter, you should be able to:

- apply the Z notation to modelling the state of more complex systems using combinations of mathematical structures;
- specify more challenging operations;
- appreciate the need to validate your specifications to ensure they are a true description of the required system;
- recognise situations in which it is desirable to define a new operator, or to name subexpressions using **let**, to enhance the readability of a specification.

11.1 Introduction

In this chapter, we will outline the construction of two Z specifications. The specifications are incomplete and not very large, but they are a little more challenging than the examples we have encountered so far, and should illustrate the value of Z in expressing complex ideas clearly and precisely.

11.2 A timetabling system

A university requires a timetabling system to keep track of where and when its degree modules are scheduled, and which students are registered for each module. Sometimes a module can be scheduled in several rooms at the same time, perhaps for tutorial sessions in smaller groups, in which case we wish to know which room any given student should be in. We could visualise the final system as an on-line facility by which students can find out where they should be at any given time, register for modules, find out where their friends will be, etc. For simplicity, we will say that a given student may attend any number of modules provided none of their chosen modules clash on the timetable, and we will assume that there is no limit on the capacity of rooms or the number of students permitted to register for a module. For the time being, we will also ignore the role of lecturers and tutorial staff in the specification!

For our preliminary analysis, we identify the basic types (given sets) necessary for the specification. We will assume that for the purpose of time-tabling, the week is divided into fixed-size time slots in which modules may be scheduled. This suggests the following basic types:

$$[STUDENT, MODULE, TIMESLOT, ROOM]$$

which are respectively the set of all students, the set of all modules, the set of all time slots and the set of all teaching rooms.

The time slots could be units of one hour, two hours, half a day, or what-ever. Making *TIMESLOT* a basic type means that we do not need to concern ourselves with the precise nature of a time slot at our chosen level of abstraction.

We must now describe the abstract state of the system using appropriate mathematical structures. Clearly, there is more than one way of doing this, but the one we will choose is based on the idea that each individual student and each individual module will be associated with their/its own individual schedule. This models the real-world situation, where each student will carry around their personal schedule, and a module lecturer might issue a schedule for his/her module. We can model a schedule as a relation between time slots and rooms. However, for any given time slot, a given student can only be in a maximum of one room (one cannot be in two places at the same time!), so therefore a student's schedule will be a *partial function* from time slots to rooms. Therefore, the type of a student's schedule will be

$$TIMESLOT \nrightarrow ROOM$$

and the type of a module's schedule will be

$$TIMESLOT \leftrightarrow ROOM$$

Now, we need a way to represent the schedules for *all* students and *all* modules on the course. We can do this using two partial functions, one of which maps individual students to their schedules, and the other of which maps individual modules to their schedules. These functions are called *studentTT* and *moduleTT* respectively.

$$studentTT: STUDENT \nrightarrow (TIMESLOT \nrightarrow ROOM)$$
$$moduleTT: MODULE \nrightarrow (TIMESLOT \leftrightarrow ROOM)$$

studentTT s is the schedule for student *s*, and *moduleTT m* is the schedule for module *m*.

dom *studentTT*

is the set of all students on the course and

dom *moduleTT*

is the set of all modules which may be offered on the course. However, not all students are registered for modules and not all modules are offered at any given time. For a student *s* not registered for any modules,

$$studentTT s = \varnothing$$

and for a module *m* not currently offered,

$$moduleTT m = \varnothing$$

that is, *s* and *m* are mapped to empty schedules.

These structures constitute the state declarations for the specification. We must now identify the invariant properties required to define the state predicate:

1. It must not be possible to have two modules scheduled in the same room at the same time; in other words, the relations (schedules) in the range of *moduleTT* must be disjoint.

    $$\forall r, s : \text{ran } moduleTT \bullet \text{disjoint } \langle r, s \rangle$$

    The predicate implies that no two module schedules have any maplets in common; that is, no two modules are scheduled in the same room at the same time.

2. A student can only be scheduled for a time and place where a module is scheduled. In other words, any maplet found in any of the functions in the range of *studentTT* must also be found in precisely one of the relations in the range of *moduleTT*.

    To express this requirement in Z, we need a convenient way of referring to the set of *all* the maplets in the ranges of *studentTT* and of *moduleTT* respectively. We will define a generic global constant function *allPairs*, which when applied to objects such as *studentTT* or *moduleTT* returns the distributed union of all the relations in the object's range. (See Section 9.4 for a description of generic constants.)

$$
\begin{array}{l}
\text{———} [X, Y, Z] \text{———} \\
\hline
allPairs : (X \rightarrow\!\!\!\!\!\rightarrow (Y \leftrightarrow Z)) \rightarrow (Y \leftrightarrow Z) \\
\hline
\forall f : (X \rightarrow\!\!\!\!\!\rightarrow (Y \leftrightarrow Z)) \bullet \\
allPairs\ f = \bigcup \{x : X \mid x \in \text{dom } f \bullet fx\}
\end{array}
$$

For example, say *studentTT* has the following value:

$$
\begin{aligned}
studentTT = \{ &sally \mapsto \{t_1 \mapsto r_4, t_3 \mapsto r_4, t_5 \mapsto r_1\}, \\
&helen \mapsto \{t_2 \mapsto r_1, t_3 \mapsto r_4\}, \\
&john \mapsto \{t_1 \mapsto r_1, t_5 \mapsto r_2\} \\
&\}
\end{aligned}
$$

then

$$allPairs\ studentTT = \{t_1 \mapsto r_4, t_3 \mapsto r_4, t_5 \mapsto r_1, t_2 \mapsto r_1, t_1 \mapsto r_1, t_5 \mapsto r_2\}$$

Condition 2 can now be expressed as

$$allPairs\ studentTT \subseteq allPairs\ moduleTT$$

Note that this predicate simply states that every maplet in every student's schedule also occurs in the schedule of *at least* one module. The additional constraint that each student schedule maplet is in the schedule of *precisely one* module is implied by the predicate for condition 1.

Here is our final condition.

3. Any given student is either scheduled to attend a given module at every available time slot, or not at all. Although this is a valid requirement for our specification, it may not be reflected in the behaviour of real students!

$$
\begin{aligned}
&\forall s : \text{dom } studentTT;\ m : \text{dom } moduleTT \\
&\bullet (studentTT\ s \cap moduleTT\ m) \neq \varnothing \Rightarrow \\
&\quad \text{dom}(studentTT\ s \cap moduleTT\ m) = \text{dom}(moduleTT\ m)
\end{aligned}
$$

The expression

$$(studentTT\ s \cap moduleTT\ m) \neq \varnothing$$

is true iff student s and module m are scheduled to be in the same place at the same time on at least one occasion. The expression

$$\mathrm{dom}(studentTT\, s \cap moduleTT\, m) = \mathrm{dom}(moduleTT\, m)$$

states that student s is scheduled to attend module m at all of the times when the module is available.

The state schema for our system is therefore

```
_____ Timetable _____
studentTT: STUDENT ↦ (TIMESLOT ↦ ROOM )
moduleTT: MODULE ↦ (TIMESLOT ↔ ROOM )
─────────────────────────────────────────────────
∀r, s : ran moduleT • disjoint⟨r, s⟩

allPairs studentTT ⊆ allPairs moduleTT

∀s : dom studentTT; m : dom moduleTT
 • (studentTT s ∩ moduleTT m) ≠ ∅ ⇒
   dom(studentTT s ∩ moduleTT m) = dom(moduleTT m)
```

For the initial state, we will have no students and no modules in the system.

```
_ InitTimetable ____
 TimeTable'
─────────────────
 studentTT' = { }
 moduleTT' = { }
```

Inspection of the system state shows that this initial state exists. (Strictly, we are obliged to verify this formally.)

We should examine our specification to see whether it has any unforeseen undesirable properties. This check could take the form of a walkthrough with colleagues, in which the group tries to find inconsistencies in the specification as a representation of the user's requirements. For example, is it possible for a student to be scheduled for two different modules which clash on the timetable; that is, which take place at the same time? The answer is no, because every student's schedule is a function.

We should also check for any particular desirable properties which we would expect the specification to have. Other questions can give us more insight into our specification. For example, if two students are never in the same place at the same time, must it be that they have no modules in common? A moment's consideration reveals that this is not necessarily true. It may be that a module has concurrent sessions in more than one room at every time slot in which it is scheduled, in which case two students could do the module without ever being in the same room.

Such checks can be made at any stage in the development of the specification, but it is a good idea to find any errors in the state specification before embarking on operation specifications.

The use of implication $\Rightarrow$ is a common source of errors, and it is a good idea to check that the correct meaning has been captured. In condition 3, for example, what have we said about the following situation?

$$(studentTT\,s \cap moduleTT\,m) = \varnothing$$

In fact, dom $\varnothing = \varnothing$ (Spivey 1992), and so the consequent (right-hand side of $\Rightarrow$) will be true iff $moduleTT\,m = \varnothing$, that is module m is not timetabled, and false otherwise; either way the predicate will be true.

Validation exercises are not guaranteed to reveal all inconsistencies in the specification, but the fact that the specification is expressed in a formal language makes it easier to identify such inconsistencies. Verification by formal proof gives more confidence, but is much more expensive in time and effort.

Exercises 11.1

1. What assumption is implicit in condition 3 of the state invariant?
2. What issues would have to be considered in order to introduce the concept of *lecturers* for the modules? For example, what assumptions must you make about the case where a module is scheduled in more than one room at the same time?

Adding a student to the course

The student $s?$ must not already be on the course.

$$s? \notin \text{dom } studentTT$$

The student joins the course with an initially empty schedule.

$$studentTT' = studentTT \cup \{s? \mapsto \varnothing\}$$

The operation schema is as follows:

```
_____ AddStudent _____
Δ Timetable
s?: STUDENT
_____
s? ∉ dom studentTT
studentTT' = studentTT ∪ {s? ↦ ∅}
moduleTT' = moduleTT
```

Exercises 11.2

1. Write the operation schema *AddModule*, to add a module with an empty schedule to the system.
2. Write the operation schemas *RemoveStudent* and *RemoveModule*.

Scheduling a module

The module *m?* must be a valid module for the course

$m? \in dom\ moduleTT$

and it must not already be scheduled:

$moduleTT\ m? = \emptyset$

The postcondition is non-deterministic in that more than one valid potential schedule for the module may be possible, and in these circumstances, the postcondition does not state which valid schedule is to be selected. This arbitrary decision is left to the implementors of the system. Thus the schema defines more than one possible final state.

$\exists\ schedule: TIMESLOT \leftrightarrow ROOM \bullet$
$(allPairs\ moduleTT \cap schedule = \emptyset$
$\wedge\ moduleTT' = moduleTT \oplus \{m? \mapsto schedule\})$

The components of this predicate are explained as follows. Any valid schedule for this module must not clash with that of any other module.

$allPairs\ moduleTT \cap schedule = \emptyset$

The module is scheduled by overriding the *moduleTT* function.

$moduleTT' = moduleTT \oplus \{m? \mapsto schedule\}$

The operation schema is as follows:

```
┌─────── ScheduleModule ───────────────────
│ Δ Timetable
│ m?: MODULE
├──────────────────────────────────────────
│ m? ∈ dom moduleTT
│ moduleTT m? = ∅
│ ∃ schedule: TIMESLOT ↔ ROOM •
│   (allPairs moduleTT ∩ schedule = ∅
│    ∧ moduleTT' = moduleTT ⊕ {m? ↦ schedule})
│
│ studentTT' = studentTT
└──────────────────────────────────────────
```

Descheduling a module

The module to be descheduled $m?$ must be a valid module for the course.

$$m? \in \text{dom } moduleTT$$

and the schedule for $m?$ must not already be empty.

$$moduleTT\, m? \neq \emptyset$$

To deschedule the module, we override $moduleTT$ to map the module to the empty schedule.

$$moduleTT' = moduleTT \oplus \{m? \mapsto \emptyset\}$$

We must also remove the module from the schedules of all students who are registered for it.

$$studentTT' = \bigcup\{s: \text{dom } studentTT \bullet \{s \mapsto (studentTT\, s \setminus moduleTT\, m?)\}\}$$

The operation schema is as follows:

```
┌─────── DescheduleModule ──────────────────
│ Δ Timetable
│ m?: MODULE
├──────────────────────────────────────────
│ m? ∈ dom moduleTT
│ moduleTT m? ≠ ∅
│ moduleTT' = moduleTT ⊕ {m? ↦ ∅}
│ studentTT' = ∪{s: dom studentTT • {s ↦ (studentTT s \ moduleTT m?)}}
└──────────────────────────────────────────
```

Note that the precondition *moduleTT m?* $\neq \emptyset$ is not necessary for the operation as specified, but it may be important to identify it at implementation, to output an appropriate message if the precondition is not satisfied. This exception would be handled by a separate schema, and the total operation would be specified using schema calculus.

Registering a student for a module

The student *s?* must be on the course, and the module *m?* must be a valid module for the course.

$s? \in \text{dom } studentTT$
$m? \in \text{dom } moduleTT$

The module must be scheduled.

$moduleTT\, m? \neq \emptyset$

The student must be free at all the times when the module is scheduled.

$\text{dom}(studentTT\, s?) \cap \text{dom}(moduleTT\, m?) = \emptyset$

We do not want to add all the module's slots to the student's schedule; where the module is scheduled in more than one room at the same time, the student must be allocated only one of these slots. The following postcondition predicate is non-deterministic in this respect, in that it does not state specifically which slot is to be allocated in these circumstances. (In a real system, issues such as room capacities and previous allocations would come into play.) The postcondition is as follows:

$\exists\, newPairs : TIMESLOT \rightarrow ROOM$
$\bullet\; ((\text{dom } newPairs = \text{dom } moduleTT\, m?)$
$\quad \wedge (newPairs \subseteq moduleTT\, m?)$
$\quad \wedge (studentTT' = studentTT \oplus \{s? \mapsto studentTT\, s? \cup newPairs\}))$

newPairs is the set of those pairs from the module's schedule which are to be added to the student's schedule. Note that because students' schedules are functions, *newPairs* must be a function. The constituent parts of this predicate are explained as follows.

The time slots for the pairs to be added to the student's schedule are precisely *all* the time slots when the module is available.

$\text{dom } newPairs = \text{dom } moduleTT\, m?$

The pairs to be added to the student's schedule are pairs from the module's schedule.

$newPairs \subseteq moduleTT\, m?$

The appropriate pairs are added to the student's schedule by overriding the *studentTT* function.

$studentTT' = studentTT \oplus \{s? \mapsto studentTT\, s? \cup newPairs\}$

The operation schema is as follows:

$$\begin{array}{l}
\underline{\qquad\qquad RegForModule \qquad\qquad\qquad\qquad\qquad} \\
\Delta\ Timetable \\
s? : STUDENT \\
m? : MODULE \\
\hline
s? \in \mathrm{dom}\ studentTT \\
m? \in \mathrm{dom}\ moduleTT \\
moduleTT\, m? \neq \varnothing \\
\mathrm{dom}(studentTT\, s?) \cap \mathrm{dom}(moduleTT\, m?) = \varnothing \\
\\
\exists\ newPairs : TIMESLOT \nrightarrow ROOM \\
\bullet\ ((\mathrm{dom}\ newPairs = \mathrm{dom}\ moduleTT\, m?) \\
\quad \wedge\ (newPairs \subseteq moduleTT\, m?) \\
\quad \wedge\ (studentTT' = studentTT \oplus \{s? \mapsto studentTT\, s? \cup newPairs\})) \\
\\
moduleTT' = moduleTT
\end{array}$$

Exercises 11.3

1. Write a schema to 'deregister' a student from a module.
2. How could we modify the state schema to specify that each module can use a maximum of one room in any given time slot?
3. How could we modify the state schema to specify that each module is only allowed one time slot in the schedule?
4. Write a Z expression for the set of all students registered for a module *m*.
5. Write a Z expression for the set of all modules being taken by a student *s*.
6. Write a Z expression for the set of all students in a room *r* at a time *t*.
7. Write a Z expression for the set of all modules which student *p* and student *q* have in common.
8. Write a Z expression for the set of all times when student *p* and student *q* are in the same room.

9. Write a Z expression for the set of all modules which clash with a module *m* on the timetable, that is which take place at the same time as module *m*.

10. Write a Z expression for the set of all time/room maplets for which one or more modules are scheduled, but no students are scheduled.

11. What would it mean if *allPairs moduleTT* was one-to-one? (See Section 7.4 for a definition of the term one-to-one for functions.)

12. What would it mean if *allPairs studentTT* was one-to-one?

13. How could you extend the specification to include concepts such as room capacities and maximum numbers of students allowed in a module.

14. Why would it be difficult to extend the module registration example in Chapter 6 to include timetabling information?

11.3 A genealogical database

A database is required to keep track of genealogical relationships between people (family trees). It would be possible to represent the required relationships (parent, grandparent, aunt, cousin, etc.) separately, but this would limit the number of relationships, increase the complexity of the specification, and would make it necessary to carry out extensive integrity checks every time the database is updated. We will therefore represent only the minimum information necessary to be able to define operations to output any required relationships. The most fundamental genealogical relationship is that of parent to child, and this, together with the sex of all the individuals in the database, will be enough to enable us to specify all the operations we require. This suggests the following types:

$[PERSON]$ the set of all people
$GENDER ::= male \mid female$

The parent/child relationship can be represented by the relation

$parent : PERSON \leftrightarrow PERSON$

where

$x \mapsto y \in parent$

represents the information that y is x's parent.

The sex of all the people in the database can be represented by the function

$sex : PERSON \nrightarrow GENDER$

where

dom *sex*

is the set of all people in the database. A person can be in the database even if they do not occur in *parent*. It may be that information about their parents or children is not available or is incomplete.

sex p

is the sex of person *p*.

We need an invariant predicate to state that the relation *parent* only holds information about people in the database.

dom *parent* ∪ ran *parent* ⊆ dom *sex*

We also need an invariant predicate to capture such requirements as:

1. If *y* is *x*'s parent, then *x* cannot be *y*'s parent.
2. If *y* is *x*'s parent, then *y* cannot also be an ancestor of *x* at a depth in the family tree greater than that of parent, that is *y* cannot be *x*'s grandparent, great-grandparent, etc.
3. A person cannot be their own parent.

We can neatly capture all of these requirements in a predicate which states that a person cannot be their own ancestor. (You may have to think about this to convince yourself that it is true.) Now the transitive closure of *parent*

parent$^+$

will relate any person to their ancestors (parents, grandparents, great-grandparents, etc.). The required predicate is therefore simply

$\forall p : PERSON \bullet p \mapsto p \notin parent^+$

The final restriction is that anyone in the database can have a maximum of two parents, and if they have two, the parents must be of opposite sexes!

$\forall p, q, r : PERSON \bullet \{p \mapsto q, p \mapsto r\} \subseteq parent \land q \neq r \Rightarrow sex\, q \neq sex\, r$

Note that the condition restricts the number of parents to a maximum of two because the type *GENDER* only has two values.

The state schema is as follows:

```
___ GenDB _____
  parent : PERSON ↔ PERSON
  sex : PERSON ⇸ GENDER
───────────────────────────────────────────────────
  dom parent ∪ ran parent ⊆ dom sex
  ∀p : PERSON • p ↦ p ∉ parent⁺
  ∀p, q, r : PERSON • {p ↦ q, p ↦ r} ⊆ parent ∧ q ≠ r ⇒ sex q ≠ sex r
```

You may notice that there is no requirement for a person's parents to come from the same generation as each other; nor does the database contain any information about whether the people it contains are alive or dead. Thus a person in the database could have Julius Caesar as one parent and Joan of Arc as the other. However, for simplicity, we will quietly ignore this.

For the initial state, we will have an empty database.

```
__ InitGenDB __
  GenDB'
────────────────
  sex' = ∅
  parent' = ∅
```

The predicate *parent'* = ∅ is not strictly necessary, as it is implied by the state invariant, but increases the clarity of the specification. The initial state satisfies the state invariant.

Operations to change the database

The users of the database will be able to modify the information it contains using operations to add a person to the database, remove a person from the database, add or remove a parent/offspring relationship to/from the database, change the name of a person in the database, and change the sex of a person in the database.

Adding a person to the database

The inputs are a person and their sex.

```
  name? : PERSON
  morf? : GENDER
```

The person *name?* must not already be in the database.

```
  name? ∉ dom sex
```

We add them to the *sex* function.

$$sex' = sex \cup \{name? \mapsto morf?\}$$

The operation schema is as follows:

```
┌─── AddPerson ──────────────
│ Δ GenDB
│ name? : PERSON
│ morf? : GENDER
├───────────────────────────
│ name? ∉ dom sex
│ sex' = sex ∪ {name? ↦ morf?}
│ parent' = parent
└───────────────────────────
```

Exercise 11.4

Write a schema for an operation to remove a person from the database.

Adding a parent/offspring relationship to the database

The inputs are a potential offspring and a potential parent.

$$off?, par? : PERSON$$

The potential offspring and parent must be in the database

$$\{off?, par?\} \subseteq dom\ sex$$

and must not already be a maplet in *parent*, in either order.

$$off? \mapsto par? \notin parent$$
$$par? \mapsto off? \notin parent$$

There must not be more than one parent already in the database for the potential offspring

$$\#(\{off?\} \lhd parent) \leqslant 1$$

and if there is one such parent, their sex must not be the same as the new potential parent.

$$\forall x : PERSON \bullet off? \mapsto x \in parent \Rightarrow sex\ x \neq sex\ par?$$

For the postcondition, we simply add the new maplet to the relation *parent*.

$$parent' = parent \cup \{off? \mapsto par?\}$$

The operation schema is as follows:

```
┌─── AddRel ─────────────────────────────┐
│ Δ GenDB                                 │
│ off?, par? : PERSON                     │
├─────────────────────────────────────────┤
│ {off?, par?} ⊆ dom sex                  │
│ off? ↦ par? ∉ parent                    │
│ par? ↦ off? ∉ parent                    │
│ #({off?} ◁ parent) ⩽ 1                  │
│ ∀x : PERSON • off? ↦ x ∈ parent ⇒ sex x ≠ sex par? │
│ parent' = parent ∪ {off? ↦ par?}        │
│ sex' = sex                              │
└─────────────────────────────────────────┘
```

Exercise 11.5

Write a schema for an operation to remove a parent/offspring relationship from the database.

Changing the name of a person in the database

This is a rather artificial example, as we will now have to describe the type *PERSON* as the set of all people's names, which implies that all names are unique. In a real system, *PERSON* would have to be implemented as a set of unique identifiers of some sort, and for simplicity, when we refer to a 'name', we will take it to mean one of these identifiers. The inputs are the old name and the new name.

$$old?, new? : PERSON$$

The old name must be in the database, and the new one must not.

$$old? \in dom\ sex$$
$$new? \notin dom\ sex$$

The old name must be replaced by the new one in the *sex* function

$$sex' = (\{old?\} ◁ sex) \cup \{new? \mapsto sex\ old?\}$$

and all relationships involving the old name must be modified to use the new name.

$$parent' = (\{old?\} \lhd parent \rhd \{old?\})$$
$$\cup \{x:PERSON \mid x \in parent\ (\{old?\}) \bullet new? \mapsto x\}$$
$$\cup \{x:PERSON \mid x \in parent^{-1}\ (\{old?\}) \bullet x \mapsto new?\}$$

The operation schema is as follows:

__ *ChangeName* _____

$\Delta\ GenDB$
$old?, new? : PERSON$

$old? \in \text{dom}\ sex$
$new? \notin \text{dom}\ sex$
$sex' = (\{old?\} \lhd sex) \cup \{new? \mapsto sex\ old?\}$
$parent' = (\{old?\} \lhd parent \rhd \{old?\})$
$\qquad \cup \{x:PERSON \mid x \in parent\ (\{old?\}) \bullet new? \mapsto x\}$
$\qquad \cup \{x:PERSON \mid x \in parent^{-1}\ (\{old?\}) \bullet x \mapsto new?\}$

Changing the sex of a person in the database

The person $p?$ must be in the database.

At first sight, this operation would appear to require a simple overriding of the *sex* function. However, the tricky part in specifying the operation is that the person may be recorded as a *parent* in the database, that is they may be a member of ran *parent*. This means that the sex recorded for other people may have to change in order to maintain the integrity of the database, that is so that the database will not contain children with two mothers or two fathers.

An implementation of the operation would probably ask the user whether s/he wished to proceed in these circumstances, as it is unlikely that s/he would wish to make such changes simply to maintain the integrity of the database. It is much more likely that the proposed change was not correct in the first place. However, we will specify a rather contrived operation which simply makes the necessary changes. Essentially, any people with whom our person has had children must change their sex, as must anyone who has had children with those people, and so on, to ensure that anyone with two parents in the database has one of each sex.

Now the relation

$$parent^{-1}\,;parent$$

relates together people who have had children with each other. The transitive closure of this relation

$$(parent^{-1}\,;parent)^{+}$$

is the relation such that

$$p \mapsto q \in (parent^{-1}\,;parent)^{+}$$

iff p has had children with q, or p has had children with someone who has had children with q, or p has had children with someone who has had children with someone who has had children with q, ... well, you get the idea. The relational image in this relation of the set consisting solely of our person p? gives the set of all people who must have their sex changed by this operation.

$$(parent^{-1}\,;parent)^{+}\ (\{p?\})$$

We can now use this to specify a function mapping these people to the opposite sex from that given them by the *sex* function, and finally use this function to override the original *sex* function. The resulting postcondition is as follows:

$$sex' = sex \oplus$$
$$\{q : PERSON; s : GENDER \mid (q \in (parent^{-1}\,;parent)^{+}\ (\{p?\}))$$
$$\wedge (s \neq sex\ q) \bullet q \mapsto s\}$$

Note that the relation $parent^{-1}\,;parent$ also relates every parent to themselves, which enables the postcondition to specify the sex change for p? him/herself.

The operation schema is as follows:

```
┌─── ChangeSex ─────────────────────────────
│ Δ GenDB
│ p? : PERSON
├────────────────────────────────────────────
│ p? ∈ dom sex
│ sex' = sex ⊕
│   {q : PERSON; s : GENDER | (q ∈ (parent⁻¹ ; parent)⁺ ({p?}))
│     ∧ (s ≠ sex q) • q ↦ s}
│
│ parent' = parent
└────────────────────────────────────────────
```

We also require query operations to interrogate the database for information about various relationships. The next set of exercises gives you the opportunity to specify some, after which we conclude with an operation to find the common ancestors of two given people, and an operation to find the set of all cousins of specified type and removedness for a given person.

Exercises 11.6

1. Specify an operation to return the set of all people who have any one of the following relationships to a given person $x?$. The name of the required relationship should be an input to the operation.

   (i)   The parents of person $x?$.
   (ii)   The grandparents of person $x?$.
   (iii)   The grandchildren of person $x?$.
   (iv)   The descendants of person $x?$.
   (v)   The siblings of person $x?$.
   (vi)   The aunts of person $x?$.

2. Give a Z expression for the set of all people in the database who have no relatives in the database.

3. Give a Z expression for the set of all people in the database who have no siblings in the database.

4. Specify an operation to output the number of generations through which a given individual p can trace his/her family history in the database.

The common ancestors of two given people

This operation must return the set $cas!$ containing the common ancestors of two people, say $p?$ and $q?$. We will further stipulate that the set contains only the common ancestors of minimum degree, where the degree refers to the number of steps in the path up and/or down the family tree between the two people. For example, if $p?$ and $q?$ are siblings, the degree is 2. If $p?$ and $q?$ are first cousins, the degree is 4. If $p?$ is the grandparent of $q?$, the degree is 2.

The precondition is that all the people involved are in the database.

$$\{p?, q?\} \cup cas! \subseteq \text{dom } sex$$

The postcondition characterises elements of the set of common ancestors of minimum degree as people for whom there are multiple compositions of *parent* which map both $p?$ and $q?$ to them, and furthermore there are no other common ancestors with degree smaller than that of members of this set.

$$cas! = \{ca : PERSON \mid \exists m, n : \mathbb{N} \bullet$$
$$((p? \mapsto ca \in parent^n \wedge q? \mapsto ca \in parent^m)$$
$$\wedge \neg \exists r : PERSON; x, y : \mathbb{N} \bullet$$
$$((x + y < m + n) \wedge p? \mapsto r \in parent^x \wedge q? \mapsto r \in parent^y))\}$$

The operation schema is as follows:

```
_____ CommonAncestors _____
Ξ GenDB
p?, q? : PERSON
cas! : ℙ PERSON
_____
{p?, q?} ∪ cas! ⊆ dom sex

cas! = {ca : PERSON | ∃m, n : ℕ •
        (( p? ↦ ca ∈ parent^n ∧ q? ↦ ca ∈ parent^m)
        ∧ ¬∃r : PERSON; x, y : ℕ •
            ((x + y < m + n) ∧ p? ↦ r ∈ parent^x ∧ q? ↦ r ∈ parent^y))}
_____
```

Note that the specification allows for the special case where one of the two people is a direct descendant of the other, in which case the common ancestor is the person higher in the family tree. m and n are natural numbers, and it is therefore possible for either or both to be zero, yielding the identity relation on *PERSON*. The only debate might be as to whether a person can be their own ancestor!

The cousins of a given person

This operation returns the set *cousins!* containing all cousins of a given type and removedness for a given person, say $p?$. Cousins are people who have a common ancestor who is more distant than a parent, and who are not siblings. The type of cousinship is determined by the shortest path from the common ancestor to either one of the cousins. For example, for first cousins the common ancestor would be a grandparent of one cousin, for second cousins a great-grandparent, and so on. 'Removed' refers to the difference in the number of steps in the path from each cousin to the common ancestor. 'Once removed' means a difference of one step, 'twice removed' means a difference of two steps, etc. For example, my first cousins' children are my first cousins once removed, and their children are my first cousins twice removed.

This operation has an input $nth? : ℕ_1$, to represent the type of cousinship, and an input $rem? : ℕ$, to represent how far removed the relationship is. $nth?$ has type $ℕ_1$ because the minimum type of cousinship is first cousins, represented by the number 1.

The precondition simply states that everyone involved is in the database:

$\{p?\} ∪ cousins! ⊆ dom\ sex$

For the postcondition we define a relation which maps a cousin to his/her cousins at the same or a lower level in the family tree. Remember that $nth?$ is defined with respect to the cousin with the shortest path to the common ancestor, and *rem*? represents the difference in length between the two paths. The required relation is

$$(parent^{nth?+1} \mathbin{;} (parent^{-1})^{nth?+1+rem?}) \setminus (parent \mathbin{;} parent^{-1})$$

The set subtraction removes from the relation all pairs of people who have the same parents. Therefore if *rem*? is zero, the relation does not relate anyone to themselves or their siblings.

The image of our person in this relation will yield all the relevant cousins at the same or a lower level in the family tree as our person. However, if the value of *rem*? is non-zero, our person may have some cousins with the same relationship at a higher level in the tree. We therefore also require the image of our person in the *inverse* of the above relation. To avoid repeating the expression for this relation, we use a Z construct called a *let predicate* which provides a method for naming subexpressions in complex predicates.

let $n == e \bullet p$

stands for the predicate p, but wherever the name n occurs in p, it represents the value e. We use a let predicate to give the name *cosrel* to the above relation for use as a subexpression in specifying the set of all *nth*? cousins *rem*? removed, both above and below person p? in the family tree.

The operation schema is as follows:

┌─── *Cousins* ──────────────────────────────────
│ Ξ *GenDB*
│ $p?: PERSON$
│ $nth?: \mathbb{N}_1$
│ $rem?: \mathbb{N}$
│ $cousins!: \mathbb{P}\ PERSON$
├──
│ $\{p?\} \cup cousins! \subseteq \mathrm{dom}\ sex$
│
│ **let** $cosrel == (parent^{nth?+1} \mathbin{;} (parent^{-1})^{nth?+1+rem?}) \setminus (parent \mathbin{;} parent^{-1}) \bullet$
│ $\quad cousins! = cosrel(\{p?\}) \cup cosrel^{-1}(\{p?\})$
└──

11.4 In conclusion

In this chapter, we have looked at two outline specifications which are somewhat more complex than those we have met previously. However, we have not introduced much new notation; we have simply applied our previous knowledge to some harder problems. Hopefully these examples will serve to demonstrate the power of the Z notation to model complex situations succinctly, clearly and precisely. If you are having difficulty understanding them, it may help to draw pictures of typical values of the state variables, to enable you to visualise what is going on. If you understand the examples at first viewing that's fine, but if not, don't be disheartened! Complex problems require a lot of study, and if it was easy it wouldn't be rewarding. When you can understand, modify and extend the above examples, you will be very well prepared for further study of the Z language.

CHAPTER 12

Further study

Aims

To provide some pointers to more advanced study of Z, and some places to look for further information about Z and its applications.

Learning objectives

When you have completed this chapter, you should:

- be aware of some more advanced aspects of Z and where to find out more about them;
- know where to look to find out about the use of Z on real projects;
- know how to contact other Z users, and how to find out about forthcoming Z conferences.

12.1 The end of the beginning?

If you have read the preceding chapters and tried the exercises, you should have acquired the solid basic knowledge and skills necessary for constructing your own Z specifications. However, I hope you have been motivated to take your study of Z further, and in this chapter I outline some ways in which you can do this.

12.2 Proof

The common perception that formal specification is about proof is probably a major reason why it has not been more widely adopted. As we have demonstrated, the use of a formal notation for writing specifications has many benefits, even if no proof is undertaken. However, the use of proof has several important uses in formal specification. Proof can give us more confidence in our specification by allowing us to verify that the specification possesses some desired property. Strictly, we should always determine that the proposed initial state for a specification actually exists, by proving an initialisation theorem. We can use proof in precondition analysis to simplify precondition schemas and determine the states in which an operation may take place, and whether it is total.

Z allows the developer to create a specification at a high level of abstraction, and incrementally to refine it, increasing the level of detail, until the specification can easily be implemented in a programming language. This refinement will involve so-called reification of our state data; that is, representing more abstract structures with more concrete ones. For example, we might represent a set as a sequence, which could then be implemented as an array in the target language. We would also have to decompose the operations of the specification to operate on the less abstract state, thus making them less abstract, more algorithmic, and therefore easier to implement in the final program. This process of refinement can make the solution of complex problems more tractable. However, it places obligations on us to prove that each refinement is correct: that is, that it is consistent with and displays the same behaviour as the more abstract version.

Diller (1994) contains an introduction to proof techniques and their application in specifications. Woodcock and Davies (1996) contains a good treatment of refinement. As a final point, it should be noted that proof may be used to a greater or lesser extent in formal specifications, from rigorous argument to completely formal proof. As stated in Woodcock and Davies (1996), 'techniques involving proof are successful where formal methods are used with a light touch, and where proofs are conducted at an appropriate level of formality'.

12.3 Animation

Animation is the translation of a specification into a programming language, so that it may be executed with different inputs. In effect, animation allows us to test the specification to give more confidence that it is a correct description of the user's requirements; we create a specification-level prototype which the developers and the client can play around with. Although this may be expensive in terms of resources, it may be justified by the importance of the individual project. Animation can help us where proof cannot, in checking that we have correctly translated informally expressed user requirements into a formal specification. Typically, declarative languages are chosen for animation. For example, Diller (1994) discusses the animation of Z specifications using Prolog and Miranda. However, Z specifications are often (quite rightly) highly abstract in nature and do not necessarily translate directly into an executable form in another language, and it is important that any compromises necessary to effect the translation do not result in behaviour different from that of the original specification.

12.4 Object orientation in Z

The object-oriented development paradigm is a natural extension of the programming concepts of modularisation and abstract data types. An object provides a means of encapsulating some data together with the operations (methods) allowable on that data. An object-oriented program consists of a collection of objects, which perform a required task by sending messages to each other. The messages are calls to the objects' methods. The nature of the objects in the program is defined using classes, which are an extension of the concept of types. Specifications written in standard Z do not always map neatly onto implementations in the object-oriented paradigm. This is a serious drawback, as the future in software development would appear to be object oriented. (Currently the object-oriented language C++ is widely used in the software industry, but not necessarily to write object-oriented programs!) However, object-oriented styles for writing Z specifications, and many object-oriented variations of Z, have been developed, the most significant being Object-Z. Descriptions of some of them can be found in Stepney *et al.* (1992).

12.5 Z tools

There are various tools available to support Z specification, including LaTeX style files to handle Z fonts, type checkers and theorem provers. A list of some of the tools can be obtained via the Z User Group (see below).

12.6 Case studies

A good way of learning to do anything better is to study examples of good practice by others. Woodcock and Davies (1996) and Hayes (1993) contain some good case studies. Barden *et al.* (1994) also has good case studies, and much other useful material for those who wish to become practical users of Z.

12.7 Further information on Z

The Z User Group organises the annual International Conference of Z Users. To join the group, you simply subscribe to the comp.specification.z USENET newsgroup or the ZFORUM mailing list. The user group promulgates information on the meetings, has a list of frequently asked questions, and information on publications, courses, tools, the draft ISO/BSI Z standard and much other information. Contact zforum-request@comlab.ox.ac.uk for further information.

Solutions to selected exercises

Exercises 2.1

1. T, T, F, F, T (of course), F.
2. $x > 0$ is not a proposition because we cannot give it a truth value. x is a parameter; replacing x with a numerical value would yield a proposition. Such an expression is called a *predicate*.

Exercise 2.2

The connective $\vee$ is *inclusive or*; it would allow the possibility of playing both football *and* golf. The meaning of the word *or* in everyday life is usually that of *exclusive or*, that is I'll play football or golf, but not both. The truth table would be as follows:

P	Q	$P \oplus Q$
F	F	F
F	T	T
T	F	T
T	T	F

Exercises 2.3

1.
   (i) $P \vee (Q \wedge R)$ neither

P	Q	R	$Q \wedge R$	$P \vee (Q \wedge R)$
F	F	F	F	F
F	F	T	F	F
F	T	F	F	F
F	T	T	T	T
T	F	F	F	T
T	F	T	F	T
T	T	F	F	T
T	T	T	T	T

(ii) $\neg P \vee Q$ neither

(iii) $(P \Rightarrow Q) \Leftrightarrow (Q \Rightarrow P)$ neither

P	Q	P⇒Q	Q⇒P	(P ⇒ Q)⇔(Q ⇒ P)
F	F	T	T	T
F	T	T	F	F
T	F	F	T	F
T	T	T	T	T

(iv) $\neg(P \vee Q)$ neither

(v) $\neg(P \wedge \neg Q)$ neither

(vi)   *false* $\vee$ *true*   tautology

(vii)   *false* $\wedge \neg(P \vee Q)$ contradiction

P	Q	false	¬(P∨Q)	false ∧ ¬(P∨Q)
F	F	F	T	F
F	T	F	F	F
T	F	F	F	F
T	T	F	F	F

(ii) and (v) are logically equivalent.

2. $\neg R \vee (\neg S \wedge \neg P)$

Exercise 2.4

Dual of $P \vee P \Leftrightarrow P$ is $P \wedge P \Leftrightarrow P$.

Proof of $P \wedge P \Leftrightarrow P$:

$$P \wedge P$$
$$\Leftrightarrow (P \wedge P) \vee false \qquad \text{identity law}$$
$$\Leftrightarrow (P \wedge P) \vee (P \wedge \neg P) \qquad \text{complement law}$$
$$\Leftrightarrow P \wedge (P \vee \neg P) \qquad \text{distributive law}$$
$$\Leftrightarrow P \wedge true \qquad \text{complement law}$$
$$\Leftrightarrow P \qquad \text{identity law}$$

Dual of $P \vee true \Leftrightarrow true$ is $P \wedge true \Leftrightarrow true$

P	true	P∧true
F	T	T
T	T	T

Exercises 2.5

1.

(i)   Not a predicate; an arithmetic expression.

(ii)   A predicate. (Even though whatever value x takes would yield a false proposition.)

(iii) Not a valid expression.

(iv)   A predicate.

2. (i)   Not a proposition.

(ii)   F

(iv)   F

Exercise 2.6

(i)   proposition, F

(ii)   proposition, T

(iii)   proposition, T

(iv)   proposition, F

(v)   proposition, F

(vi)   proposition, T

(vii)   predicate (contains the free variable y)

Exercises 3.1

1.

(i) $\{0, 3, 6, 9\}$

(ii) $\{1, 2, 3, 4, 5\}$

(iii) $\{2, 3, 4, 5, 6, 7, 8\}$

(iv) $\{0, 1, 4, 9\}$

2.

(i) $\{x : \mathbb{N}_1 \mid x < 4\}$

(ii) $\{k : \mathbb{N} \mid k < 5 \bullet k^2\}$

(iii) $\{k : \mathbb{N} \mid k < 5 \bullet k^2 - k\}$

Exercise 3.2

(i)   T

(ii)   T

(iii)   not valid

(iv)   F

(v)   not valid
(vi)   T
(vii)   It depends on the types of the sets. If the type of the LHS is $\mathbb{P}X$ for
        some type X, and the type of the RHS is $\mathbb{P}(\mathbb{P}X)$, then the value is F,
        otherwise the expression is invalid.
(viii) not valid

Exercises 3.3

1.
    (i)   3
    (ii)   1
    (iii) 3
    (iv)   1
    (v)   0
    (vi)   1
2.
    (i)   T
    (ii)   T
    (iii) F
    (iv)   T

Exercises 3.4

1. Any set of sets of integer. For example, $\{\{-4, 42\}, \{\}, \{7, -1, 8\}\}$.
2.
    (i) $\mathbb{P}(\mathbb{P}(\mathbb{N}))$, 2
    (ii) $\mathbb{P}(\mathbb{P}(\mathbb{P}(\mathbb{N})))$, 3
    (iii) $\mathbb{P}(\mathbb{P}(\mathbb{N}))$, 4

Exercises 3.5

1.
    (i) $\{\}$
    (ii)   invalid
    (iii) $\{\}$
    (v)   invalid
2. F
3.
    (i) $\{colin\}$
    (ii) $\mathbb{P}$ *skiing*
    (iii) $\{tony, fred, alice, sarah, diana, susan, bill, henry, don, colin, carol\}$

(iv)   {*don*}

(v)   { }

(vi)   *skiing*

(vii)   {{ }, {*sarah*}, {*fred*}, {*don*}, {*sarah, fred*}, {*sarah, don*}, {*fred, don*}, {*sarah, fred, don*}}

Exercises 3.6

1.

(i) $\forall A, B : \mathbb{P}T \bullet A \cap B = \{x : T \mid x \in A \wedge x \in B\}$

(ii) $\forall A, B : \mathbb{P}T \bullet A \setminus B = \{x : T \mid x \in A \wedge x \notin B\}$

(iii) $\forall A : \mathbb{P}(\mathbb{P}T) \bullet \cup A = \{x : T \mid \exists S : A \bullet x \in S\}$

2.

(i)   *women, men* : $\mathbb{P}$ *PERSON*

   women $\cap$ *men* = { }

   women $\cup$ *men* = *PERSON*

(ii)   *marketing, personnel, production* : $\mathbb{P}$ *PERSON*

   marketing $\cap$ *personnel* = { }

   marketing $\cap$ *production* = { }

   personnel $\cap$ *production* = { }

   Note that a more succinct way of answering (i) and (ii) would be to use *partition* and *disjoint*. (See Chapter 9.)

(iii) $\#marketing \leqslant 10$

   $\#\ personnel \leqslant 10$

   $\#\ production \leqslant 10$

(iv)   *marketing* $\subseteq$ *women*

(v) $\#((marketing \cup personnel \cup production) \cap men) >$
   $\#((marketing \cup personnel \cup production) \cap women)$

3.

(i) $\#(marketing \cap personnel \cap production \cap women)$

(ii) $\#(((marketing \cap personnel) \setminus production) \cap men)$

Exercise 4.1

```
┌─── RemoveMember ──────────────
│ Δ ClubState
│ member? : STUDENT
├───────────────────────────────
│ member? ∈ badminton
│ badminton' = badminton \ {member?}
│ hall' = hall \ {member?}
└───────────────────────────────
```

Exercise 4.2

```
┌─────── LeaveHall ────────
│ Δ ClubState
│ leaver? : STUDENT
├──────────────────────────
│ leaver? ∈ hall
│ hall' = hall \ {leaver?}
│ badminton' = badminton
└──────────────────────────
```

Exercise 4.3

```
┌─────── Location ─────────────────────
│ Ξ ClubState
│ s? : STUDENT
│ report! : MESSAGE
├───────────────────────────────────────
│ s? ∈ hall ⇒ report! = inHall
│ s? ∈ badminton ∧ s? ∉ hall ⇒ report! = notInHall
│ s? ∉ badminton ⇒ report! = notMember
└───────────────────────────────────────
```

Exercises 4.4

1.

   (i)

```
┌── P ──────
│ a, b : ℤ
├───────────
│ (a = 42) ⇔
│ (a = b + 2
│    ∧ b < 10)
└───────────
```

   (ii)

```
┌── Q ──────
│ a : ℤ
│ b : ℙ ℤ
├───────────
│ (a = 42) ⇒
│ (a = 42) ∨ (42 ∈ b)
└───────────
```

(iii)   This is not a valid schema, because the name b is used in schemas B and C for variables of different types.

2.   The schema defined is the same as that which would result from including one schema in the other. Also there are no values of a and b which could make the predicate into a true proposition.

3. $\Delta ClubState \cong ClubState \wedge ClubState'$

Exercise 4.5

$MESSAGE ::= success \mid notMember \mid hallFull \mid inHall$
$SuccessMessage \cong [outcome! : MESSAGE \mid outcome! = success]$

__ NotMember __
$\Xi ClubState$
$enterer? : STUDENT$
$outcome! : MESSAGE$

$enterer? \notin badminton$
$outcome! = notMember$

__ AlreadyInHall __
$\Xi ClubState$
$enterer? : STUDENT$
$outcome! : MESSAGE$

$enterer? \in hall$
$outcome! = inHall$

__ HallFull __
$\Xi ClubState$
$outcome! : MESSAGE$

$\#hall = maxPlayers$
$outcome! = hallFull$

$TotalEnterHall \cong (EnterHall \wedge SuccessMessage)$
$\qquad \vee NotMember$
$\qquad \vee AlreadyInHall$
$\qquad \vee HallFull$

Exercise 4.6

All of the preconditions could be made implicit. The precondition

$$enterer? \in badminton$$

is implied by the postconditions and the 'before' and 'after' versions of the state invariant

$$hall \subseteq badminton$$

The precondition

$$enterer? \notin hall$$

is not necessary as long as we don't want to report an exception when we 'add' a person to *hall* who is already in the hall.

The precondition

$$\#hall < maxPlayers$$

is subsumed by the invariant

$$\#hall' \leqslant maxPlayers$$

```
┌─────────── pre EnterHall ───────────
│ ClubState
│ enterer? : STUDENT
├──────────────────────────────────────
│ ∃ badminton', hall' : ℙ STUDENT •
│   (hall' ⊆ badminton'
│   ∧ #hall' ≤ maxPlayers
│   ∧ enterer? ∈ badminton
│   ∧ enterer? ∉ hall
│   ∧ #hall < maxPlayers
│   ∧ hall' = hall ∪ {enterer?}
│   ∧ badminton' = badminton)
└──────────────────────────────────────
```

Exercises 4.7

1.

```
┌──── Fishing ────
│ pond, net : ℙ FISH
├──────────────────
│ net ⊆ pond
│ #pond ≤ maxFish
└──────────────────
```

2.

```
┌─── Catch ────────
│ Δ Fishing
│ f? : FISH
├──────────────────
│ f? ∈ pond
│ f? ∉ net
│ net' = net ∪ {f?}
│ pond' = pond
└──────────────────
```

3.

```
┌─── Return ───────
│ Δ Fishing
│ fs? : ℙ FISH
├──────────────────
│ fs? ⊆ net
│ net' = net \ fs?
│ pond' = pond
└──────────────────
```

4.

```
┌─── Stock ─────────────
│ Δ Fishing
│ fs? : ℙ FISH
├───────────────────────
│ fs? ∩ pond = { }
│ #fs? + #pond ≤ maxFish
│ pond' = pond ∪ fs?
│ net' = net
└───────────────────────
```

5.

```
┌─── FreeFish ──────────
│ Ξ Fishing
│ numFree! : ℕ
├───────────────────────
│ numFree! = #(pond \ net)
└───────────────────────
```

Exercise 6.1

(i) $\{1 \mapsto 2,\ 1 \mapsto 3\}$

(ii) $(\{\,\} \mapsto 2,\ \{\,\} \mapsto 3,\ \{1\} \mapsto 2,\ \{1\} \mapsto 3)$

(iii) $\{\{\,\},\ \{1 \mapsto 2\},\ \{1 \mapsto 3\},\ \{1 \mapsto 2,\ 1 \mapsto 3\}\}$

(iv) $\{((1 \mapsto 2) \mapsto (1 \mapsto 2)),\ ((1 \mapsto 2) \mapsto (1 \mapsto 3)),\ ((1 \mapsto 3) \mapsto (1 \mapsto 2)),$
       $((1 \mapsto 3) \mapsto (1 \mapsto 3))\}$

Exercises 6.2

1. The empty relation $\{\,\}$.
2. The Cartesian product $PERSON \times MODULE$.
3. $\{p : PERSON \mid p \in firstYear \wedge p \mapsto programming \in taking\}$

Exercises 6.3

1. $students \setminus \operatorname{dom} taking$
2. $degModules \setminus \operatorname{ran} taking$
3. $\{m : degModules \mid \#\{p : PERSON \mid p \mapsto m \in taking\} = n\}$
4. $\forall m : \operatorname{ran} taking \bullet \#\{p : PERSON \mid p \mapsto m \in taking\} \leqslant n$
5. $matches : PERSON \leftrightarrow PERSON$
    $\operatorname{dom} matches \cap \operatorname{ran} matches = \{\,\}$
    $\forall p : \operatorname{dom} matches \bullet (\exists_1 q : \operatorname{ran} matches \bullet p \mapsto q \in matches)$
    $\forall q : \operatorname{ran} matches \bullet (\exists_1 p : \operatorname{dom} matches \bullet p \mapsto q \in matches)$

Exercises 6.4

1. $taking^{-1}(\{m\})$
2. $\{p : \operatorname{dom} taking \mid taking(\{p\}) \cap taking(\{s\}) \neq \{\,\}\}$
3. $\forall m : \operatorname{ran} taking \bullet \#(taking^{-1}(\{m\})) \leqslant n$

Exercises 6.5

1.

(i)   The person to be removed must be one of our students and must
       not be taking any modules.

```
┌──────── RemoveStudent ─────────
│ Δ ModuleReg
│ p? : PERSON
├────────────────────────────────
│ p? ∈ students
│ p? ∉ dom taking
│ students' = students \ {p?}
│ degModules' = degModules
│ taking' = taking
└────────────────────────────────
```

(ii)

```
┌──── Withdraw ────────────
│ ΔModuleReg
│ p? : PERSON
│ m? : MODULE
├──────────────────────────
│ p? ∈ students
│ m? ∈ degModules
│ p? ↦ m? ∈ taking
│ taking' = taking \ {p? ↦ m?}
│ students' = students
│ degModules' = degModules
└──────────────────────────
```

(iii)

```
┌──── AddModule ───────────
│ ΔModuleReg
│ m? : MODULE
├──────────────────────────
│ m? ∉ degModules
│ degModules' = degModules ∪ {m?}
│ students' = students
│ taking' = taking
└──────────────────────────
```

(iv)

```
┌──── RemoveModule ────────
│ Δ ModuleReg
│ m? : MODULE
├──────────────────────────
│ m? ∈ degModules
│ m? ∉ ran taking
│ degModules' = degModules \ {m?}
│ students' = students
│ taking' = taking
└──────────────────────────
```

2. Schema specifying successful case of the operation:

```
┌─────── RegForModule ───────
│ Δ ModuleReg
│ p? : PERSON
│ m? : MODULE
├─────────────────────────────
│ p? ∈ students
│ m? ∈ degModules
│ p? ↦ m? ∉ taking
│ #(taking⁻¹ ({m})) < n
│ taking' = taking ∪ { p? ↦ m?}
│ students' = students
│ degModules' = degModules
└─────────────────────────────
```

Free type for error messages:

$$MESSAGE ::= success \mid notAStudent \mid invalidModule$$
$$\mid alreadyRegistered \mid moduleFull$$

Schema to report successful outcome:

$$SuccessMessage \,\widehat{=}\, [outcome! : MESSAGE \mid outcome! = success]$$

Exception handling schemas (one for each precondition):

```
┌─────── NotAStudent ───────
│ Ξ ModuleReg
│ p? : PERSON
│ outcome! : MESSAGE
├────────────────────────────
│ p? ∉ students
│ outcome! = notAStudent
└────────────────────────────
```

```
┌─────── InvalidModule ───────
│ Ξ ModuleReg
│ m? : MODULE
│ outcome! : MESSAGE
├──────────────────────────────
│ m? ∉ degModules
│ outcome! = invalidModule
└──────────────────────────────
```

```
_____ AlreadyRegistered _____
Ξ ModuleReg
p?: PERSON
m?: MODULE
outcome!: MESSAGE
─────────────────────────────
p? ↦ m? ∈ taking
outcome! = alreadyRegistered
```

```
_____ ModuleFull _____
Ξ ModuleReg
m?: MODULE
outcome!: MESSAGE
─────────────────────────────
#(taking⁻¹ ({m})) = n
outcome! = moduleFull
```

The total operation schema:

$$TotalRegForModule \mathrel{\hat{=}} (RegForModule \wedge SuccessMessage)$$
$$\vee\ NotAStudent$$
$$\vee\ InvalidModule$$
$$\vee\ AlreadyRegistered$$
$$\vee\ ModuleFull$$

Exercises 6.6

1.

(i) $\{1 \mapsto 1,\ 4 \mapsto 16,\ 5 \mapsto 25\}$
(ii) $\{3 \mapsto 9,\ 4 \mapsto 16,\ 5 \mapsto 25\}$
(iii) $\{1 \mapsto 1\}$
(iv) $\{9 \mapsto 3\}$

2.

$taking \, (\, firstYear)$
$\mathrm{ran}(\, firstYear \lhd taking)$

3. $students \setminus \mathrm{dom}(taking \rhd progMods)$

Exercises 6.7

1. $cites^+(\{x\})$
2. $\mathrm{dom}\ cites^+ \setminus \mathrm{ran}\ cites^+$

3. $\forall p,\, q : PAPER \bullet p \mapsto q \in cites^+ \Rightarrow q \mapsto p \notin cites^+$

4.

```
┌─── ModuleReg ──────────────────────────────┐
│ students : ℙ PERSON                         │
│ degModules : ℙ MODULE                       │
│ taking, completed : PERSON ↔ MODULE         │
├─────────────────────────────────────────────┤
│ dom taking ⊆ students                       │
│ ran taking ⊆ degModules                     │
│ dom completed ⊆ students                    │
│ ran completed ⊆ degModules                  │
│ ∀s : students • ({s} ◁ taking)∩({s} ◁ completed) = { } │
└─────────────────────────────────────────────┘
```

One possible new operation would be for a student to complete a module which s/he is taking.

5.

```
┌─── RegForModule ──────────┐
│ Δ ModuleReg               │
│ p? : PERSON               │
│ m? : MODULE               │
├───────────────────────────┤
│ p? ∈ students             │
│ m? ∈ degModules           │
│ p? ↦ m? ∉ taking          │
│ p? ↦ m? ∉ completed       │
│ taking' = taking ∪ { p? ↦ m?} │
│ students' = students      │
│ degModules' = degModules  │
│ completed' = completed    │
└───────────────────────────┘
```

6. We extend the state schema by including it in a new schema *ModuleRegWithPrereqs* which adds the necessary extra declarations and predicates. We introduce the relation

$$isPrereqFor : MODULE \leftrightarrow MODULE$$

where $p \mapsto q \in isPrereqFor$ means that module p is a prerequisite for module q. The predicate

$$\text{dom } isPrereqFor \cup \text{ran } isPreReqFor \subseteq degModules$$

specifies that all the modules in the relation *isPreqFor* are valid modules from our modular degree scheme. The predicate

$$\forall p, q : degModules \bullet p \mapsto q \in isPrereqFor \Rightarrow q \mapsto p \notin isPrereqFor$$

specifies that if a given module is a prerequisite for another module, then the second module cannot be a prerequisite for the first. (Note that a homogeneous relation with the above property is called an *asymmetric* relation.) The predicate

$$\forall p, q, r : degModules \bullet p \mapsto q \in isPrereqFor \land q \mapsto r \in isPrereqFor$$
$$\Rightarrow p \mapsto r \in isPrereqFor$$

specifies that if a given module is a prerequisite for another module, which in turn is prerequisite for a third module, then the first is also prerequisite for the third. (Note that a homogeneous relation with the above property is called a *transitive* relation.) Finally, the predicate

$$\forall s : students; \ p, \ q : degModules \mid p \mapsto q \in isPrereqFor$$
$$\bullet \ q \in taking(s) \Rightarrow p \in completed \ (s)$$

specifies that if a given student is taking a module for which another module is a prerequisite, then the student must have completed the prerequisite module. The modified state schema is as follows:

─────── *ModuleRegWithPrereqs* ──────────────────────────
ModuleReg
isPrereqFor : $MODULE \leftrightarrow MODULE$
───
dom *isPrereqFor* $\cup$ ran *isPreReqFor* $\subseteq$ *degModules*

$\forall p, \ q : degModules \bullet p \mapsto q \in isPrereqFor \Rightarrow q \mapsto p \notin isPrereqFor$

$\forall p, \ q, \ r : degModules \bullet p \mapsto q \in isPrereqFor \land q \mapsto r \in isPrereqFor$
$\qquad\qquad\qquad \Rightarrow p \mapsto r \in isPrereqFor$

$\forall s : students; \ p, \ q : degModules \mid p \mapsto q \in isPrereqFor$
$\qquad \bullet \ q \in taking \ (s) \Rightarrow p \in completed \ (s)$
───

Exercises 7.1

1.

    (i)   Partial
    (ii)   Not a function
    (iii)   Total (and partial)
    (iv)   Could be a partial function; it depends on the type of i.

2. h^{-1} is not a function.

3.

    (i) $S \circ R = R \,;\, S$
    (ii) $S(R(x))$
    (iii)   Quadruple

Exercises 7.2

1.

    (i) $\{2 \mapsto 7,\ 3 \mapsto 9,\ 4 \mapsto 16,\ 5 \mapsto 25\}$
    (ii) $\{9 \mapsto 3,\ 16 \mapsto 3,\ 25 \mapsto 5,\ 7 \mapsto 2,\ 17 \mapsto 4\}$
    (iii) $\{2 \mapsto 7,\ 5 \mapsto 25,\ 4 \mapsto 17\}$
    (iv)   This expression is invalid, because $f \cup g$ is not a function.
    (v) $\{9 \mapsto 16,\ 16 \mapsto 17,\ 2 \mapsto 7,\ 3 \mapsto 16,\ 4 \mapsto 17\}$

2.

    (i) $\mathrm{dom}\, f \cap \mathrm{dom}\, g = \{\,\}$
    (ii) $\mathrm{dom}\, f \cap \mathrm{dom}\, g = \{\,\}$ or $f = g$
    (iii) $f = g$
    (iv) $g = \{\,\}$

Exercises 7.3

1. $\forall b : B \bullet \exists a : \mathrm{dom}\, f \bullet f a = b$

2. The inverse is always a function.

3. The inverse is total.

4. The inverse is a bijection.

5. The function f is the identity function on the integers, mapping every integer to itself. It is injective, surjective and bijective.

7.

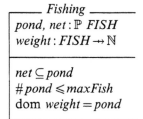

```
┌─── Fishing ───────────────
│ pond, net : ℙ FISH
│ weight : FISH ⇻ ℕ
├───────────────────────────
│ net ⊆ pond
│ #pond ⩽ maxFish
│ dom weight = pond
│
└───────────────────────────
```

```
┌─── HeaviestFish ──────────────────
│ Ξ Fishing
│ wt! : ℕ
├──────────────────────────────────
│ ∃ biggest : net | weight biggest = wt! •
│    (∀f : net • weight f ≤ weight biggest)
└
```

Note that there may be more than one 'heaviest fish' in the net. The universally quantified expression allows for this.

Exercises 8.1

1.

```
┌─── RemoveMember ──────────
│ Δ VideoShop
│ p? : PERSON
├──────────────────────────
│ p? ∈ members
│ p? ∉ dom rented
│ members' = members \ {p?}
│ rented' = rented
│ stockLevel' = stockLevel
└
```

2.

```
┌─── ReturnVideo ──────────
│ Δ VideoShop
│ p? : PERSON
│ t? : TITLE
├──────────────────────────
│ p? ∈ members
│ t? ∈ dom stockLevel
│ p? ↦ t? ∈ rented
│ rented' = rented \ {p? ↦ t?}
│ stockLevel' = stockLevel
│ members' = members
└
```

3.

```
┌─────── VideoShop ──────────────────
│ members : ℙ PERSON
│ rented : PERSON ↔ TITLE
│ stockLevel : TITLE ⇸ ℕ₁
├─────────────────────────────────────
│ dom rented ⊆ members
│ ran rented ⊆ dom stockLevel
│ ∀t : ran rented • #rented ▷ {t} ⩽ stockLevel t
│ ∀p : dom rented • #rented ({p}) ⩽ n
└─────────────────────────────────────
```

4.

```
┌─────── Renters ──────────
│ Ξ VideoShop
│ t? : TITLE
│ ps! : ℙ PERSON
├───────────────────────────
│ ps! = rented⁻¹ ({t?})
└───────────────────────────
```

5.

```
┌─────── SimilarTastes ──────────────
│ Ξ VideoShop
│ p? : PERSON
│ ps! : ℙ PERSON
├─────────────────────────────────────
│ ps! = dom rented ▷ (rented ({p?}))
└─────────────────────────────────────
```

7. The title is not already in stock, unless it is mapped to *level?*. This is implied by the fact that *stockLevel* is a function, and therefore no domain element may be mapped to more than one range element.

8. We could introduce the type

[*COPY*]   the set of all copies of videos

Now, instead of simply keeping a count of how many copies of each title we have, we can represent the *individual* copies in our specification. *rented* becomes a function from *COPY* to *PERSON*, and *stocklevel* becomes a function from *COPY* to *TITLE*, with appropriate changes to the state invariant predicates.

_____ *VideoShop* _____
members : $\mathbb{P}$ *PERSON*
rented : *COPY* $\rightarrowtail$ *PERSON*
stockLevel : *COPY* $\rightarrowtail$ *TITLE*

_____

ran *rented* $\subseteq$ *members*
dom *rented* $\subseteq$ dom *stockLevel*

This representation is more abstract and less algorithmic (less like a computer program) than the previous version. It suggests an implementation whereby the whereabouts of each *individual* copy could be tracked by the system (perhaps by barcoding), rather than the system simply knowing the number of copies in the shop and which members have a copy of each title. It also allows a given member to rent more than one copy of a title if available.

It would be a good exercise for you to write all the operation schemas again, using this new representation of the system state!

Exercises 9.1

1.

(i) $\{1 \mapsto a, 1 \mapsto d, 2 \mapsto b, 2 \mapsto e, 3 \mapsto c, 3 \mapsto f\}$
        A relation which is neither a sequence, nor a function.
(ii) $\langle a, b, c \rangle$
        A sequence
(iii) $\langle a, b \rangle$
        A sequence
(iv) $\langle a, b \rangle$
        A sequence
(v) $\langle a, b \rangle$
        A sequence
(vi) $\{2 \mapsto b, 3 \mapsto c\}$
        A function which is not a sequence.
(vii) $\langle d, e, f \rangle$
        A sequence
(viii) $\{a \mapsto d, b \mapsto e, c \mapsto f\}$
        A function which is not a sequence.
(ix) $\langle 1, 2, 3 \rangle$
        A sequence

2.

(i)   *tom*
(ii)   *harry*

3.

(i) $\langle\{ann, bill, carol\}, \{tony\}, \{joe, mary\}\rangle$

A sequence of sets of people. This example has three members.

(iv) $\langle\{\{jim, bill, carol\} \mapsto \text{ford}, \{mary\} \mapsto \text{fiat}\}, \{\{tony\} \mapsto \text{rover},$
$\{andy, mary\} \mapsto \text{volvo}\}\rangle$

A sequence of relations between sets of people and cars. This example has two members.

Exercises 9.2

1.

(i) $\langle 1, 2, 3\rangle$

(ii) $\{1, 2, 3\}$

(iii) $\{1, 2\}$

(iv) $\langle c, a, b\rangle$

(v) $\{1\}$

(vi) $\langle b\rangle$

(vii) $\{1, 3, 5\}$

(viii) 9

(ix) $\langle 1, 2, 3, 4, 1, 2\rangle$

(x) $\langle c, d, e\rangle$

(xi) $\langle 4, 3, 2\rangle$

2. $\forall i, j : \text{dom } s \bullet i < j \Rightarrow si \leqslant sj$

3.

$$
\begin{array}{|l}
\hline
\rule{0pt}{2.5ex}\text{\hspace{2em}} [X] \text{\hspace{2em}} \\
\; tail : seq_1\, X \to seq\, X \\
\hline
\; \forall s : seq_1\, X \bullet tail\, s = squash(\{1\} \lhd s) \\
\hline
\end{array}
$$

4.

$$
\begin{array}{|l}
\hline
\rule{0pt}{2.5ex}\text{\hspace{2em}} [X] \text{\hspace{2em}} \\
\; \_\, for \,\_ : seq\, X \times \mathbb{N} \to seq\, X \\
\hline
\; \forall s : seq\, X;\; n : \mathbb{N} \bullet s\, for\, n = \{1 \mathinner{.\,.} n\} \lhd s \\
\hline
\end{array}
$$

Exercises 9.3

1.

```
_____ EnterHall _____
Δ ClubState2
p? : STUDENT
──────────────────────────
p? ∈ badminton
p? ∉ hall
# hall ⩽ maxPlayers
waiting' = waiting ⌢ ⟨ p? ⟩
onCourt' = onCourt
badminton' = badminton
```

Note that the state invariant implicitly specifies the effect on the set *hall*, although it is often considered good practice, for clarity, to state explicitly the effect of an operation on all elements of the state.

2.

[CHAR]   the set of all characters
$\exists p, q : \text{seq } CHAR \bullet p \frown s \frown q = t$

3. $\#(s \triangleright \{n\})$
4.   Its range must be a prefix subset of $\mathbb{N}_1$.
5. $s = rev\, s$

Exercises 10.1

1.   dom *studInterests* = dom *allocation*
2.   dom *allocation* = { }
3.   Removing a student from the system:

```
_____ RemoveStudent _____
Δ ProjectAlloc
s? : PERSON
──────────────────────────────────
s? ∈ dom studInterests
s? ∉ dom allocation
studInterests' = {s?} ⊲ studInterests
lecInterests' = lecInterests
allocation' = allocation
placesLeft' = placesLeft
```

4. Removing a lecturer from the system:

```
_____ RemoveLecturer _____
Δ ProjectAlloc
l?: PERSON
_____
l? ∈ dom lecInterests
l? ∉ ran allocation
lecInterests' = {l?} ⩤ lecInterests
maxPlaces' = {l?} ⩤ maxPlaces
studInterests' = studInterests
allocation' = allocation
```

5. $allocation^{-1}(\{s\})$

6. $((allocation \,;\, allocation^{-1})(\{p\})) \setminus \{p\}$

Exercises 10.2

1.

```
_____ AddLecsTopic _____
Δ ProjectAlloc
l?: PERSON
t?: TOPIC
pos?: ℕ₁
_____
l? ∈ dom lecInterests
t? ∉ ran(lecInterests l?)
lecInterests' = lecInterests ⊕ {l? ↦ (0 .. pos? −1 ⩤ lecInterests l?) ⌢ ⟨t?⟩
                                   ⌢ squash( pos? .. #lecInterests l?
                                   ⩤ lecInterests l?)}
maxPlaces' = maxPlaces
studInterests' = studInterests
allocation' = allocation
```

2. The definition must capture the fact that, for a student to be a member of this set, topic t must be in the preference lists of both the student and his/her supervisor, and any topic higher in the student's preference list than t must not be in the lecturer's preference list.

$\{s: \text{dom } allocation; \; l: \text{ran } allocation; \; i: \mathbb{N} \mid i \mapsto t \in studInterests \; s$
$\qquad \wedge t \in \text{ran } lecInterests \; l \wedge s \mapsto l \in allocation$
$\qquad \wedge \text{ran}(1 .. i − 1 \vartriangleleft studInterests \; s) \cap \text{ran } lecInterests \; l = \{\}$
$\qquad\qquad \bullet s\}$

3. We can simply modify the definition of the previous answer.

$\begin{array}{|l|}
\hline
\quad\text{_____ } \textit{TopicChosen} \text{_____} \\
\Xi\, \textit{ProjectAlloc} \\
s?: \text{dom } \textit{allocation} \\
t!: TOPIC \\
\hline
\exists\, l: \text{ran } \textit{allocation};\ i: \mathbb{N} \mid i \mapsto t! \in \textit{studInterests s}? \\
\quad \wedge\, t! \in \text{ran } \textit{lecInterests } l \wedge s? \mapsto l \in \textit{allocation} \\
\quad \wedge\, \text{ran}(1\,..\,i-1 \lhd \textit{studInterests s}?) \cap \text{ran } \textit{lecInterests } l = \{\,\} \\
\hline
\end{array}$

4. For a student to have none of his/her chosen topics available, each lecturer
    must either not have any of these topics in their preference list, or must
    already have a full quota of students allocated to them.

$$\{s: \text{dom } \textit{studInterests} \mid$$
$$\qquad s \notin \text{dom } \textit{allocation}$$
$$\qquad \wedge$$
$$\qquad \forall l: \text{dom } \textit{lecInterests} \bullet$$
$$\qquad\quad \text{ran } \textit{studInterests } s \cap \text{ran } \textit{lecInterests } l = \{\,\}$$
$$\qquad\qquad \vee \#(\textit{allocation} \rhd \{l\}) = \textit{maxPlaces } l$$
$$\}$$

5.

$$\{s: \text{dom } \textit{allocation};\ t: TOPIC;\ l: \text{ran } \textit{allocation} \mid n \mapsto t \in \textit{studInterests } s$$
$$\qquad \wedge t \in \text{ran } \textit{lecInterests } l \wedge s \mapsto l \in \textit{allocation}$$
$$\qquad \wedge \text{ran}(1\,..\,n-1 \lhd \textit{studInterests s}?) \cap \text{ran } \textit{lecInterests } l = \{\,\}$$
$$\qquad\quad \bullet s\}$$

Exercise 10.3

We could define a new operation schema which allocates a student to a
supervisor when the student is added to the system. This schema can simply be
the composition of the *AddStudent* and *Allocate* schemas.

$\textit{AddStudent}\,;\textit{Allocate}$

Exercises 11.1

1. We assume that module lectures are not repeated in the schedule (owing to
    a class being too large for any available room, for example), otherwise a
    student might be compelled to attend the same lecture more than once.

2. We could introduce a variable

$$lecturerTT: STUDENT \rightarrow (TIMESLOT \rightarrow ROOM)$$

The issues include the fact that we would need to know which module slots are for lectures and which are for practical or tutorial sessions; whether or not lectures are repeated in the schedule; whether a module's lectures can take place simultaneously, requiring more than one lecturer, etc.

Exercises 11.2

1.

```
┌─────── AddModule ──────────────
│ Δ Timetable
│ m?: MODULE
├─────────────────────────────────
│ m? ∉ dom moduleTT
│ moduleTT' = moduleTT ∪ {m? ↦ ∅}
│ studentTT' = studentTT
└─────────────────────────────────
```

Exercises 11.3

1.

```
┌─────── DeregFromModule ──────────────────────────────
│ Δ Timetable
│ s?: STUDENT
│ m?: MODULE
├───────────────────────────────────────────────────────
│ s? ∈ dom studentTT
│ m? ∈ dom moduleTT
│ studentTT s? ∩ moduleTT m? ≠ ∅
│ studentTT' = studentTT ⊕ {s? ↦ studentTT s? \ moduleTT m?}
│ moduleTT' = moduleTT
└───────────────────────────────────────────────────────
```

2. Redefine *moduleTT* as

$$moduleTT: MODULE \rightarrow (TIMESLOT \rightarrow ROOM)$$

so that ran *moduleTT* is a set of functions.

3.

$$\forall m : \text{dom } moduleTT \bullet \#(\text{dom } moduleTT \ m) \leqslant 1$$

Note that dom $\{\} = \{\}$ (Spivey 1992).

4. We require the set of all students who have at least one time/room maplet in common with module m. The state invariant implies that such a student must be scheduled for the module at *all* available time slots.

$$\{s : \text{dom } studentTT \mid studentTT \ s \cap moduleTT \ m \neq \varnothing\}$$

6.

$$\{s : \text{dom } studentTT \mid t \mapsto r \in studentTT \ s\}$$

7.

$$\{m : \text{dom } moduleTT \mid studentTT \ p \cap moduleTT \ m \neq \varnothing$$
$$\wedge \ studentTT \ q \cap moduleTT \ m \neq \varnothing\}$$

8.

$$\{t : TIMESLOT \mid \exists r : ROOM \bullet t \mapsto r \in studentTT \ p$$
$$\wedge \ t \mapsto r \in studentTT \ q\}$$

9.

$$\{cm : \text{dom } moduleTT \mid \text{dom}(moduleTT \ cm) \cap \text{dom}(moduleTT \ m) \neq \varnothing\}$$

10.

$$allpairs \ moduleTT \setminus allpairs \ studentTT$$

11. No two modules could have *any* rooms or *any* times in common, and no module could be timetabled in the same room, or at the same time, more than once in the timetable. This is likely to be a very inefficient timetable!

12. Each room could only be occupied by students at one time slot in the timetable, and only one room could be occupied at any given time slot.

14. It would be difficult to extend the module registration example in Chapter 6 to include timetabling information because we have allowed modules to take place in more than one room at the same time, so that a given student's schedule is not simply the union of the schedules of the modules the student is registered for.

Exercise 11.4

```
┌─── RemovePerson ──────────────┐
│ Δ GenDB                        │
│ name? : PERSON                 │
├────────────────────────────────┤
│ name? ∈ dom sex                │
│ sex' = {name?} ⩤ sex           │
│ parent' = {name?} ⩤ parent ⩥ {name?} │
└────────────────────────────────┘
```

Exercise 11.5

```
┌─── RemoveRel ────────────┐
│ Δ GenDB                   │
│ off?, par? : PERSON       │
├───────────────────────────┤
│ off? ↦ par? ∈ parent      │
│ parent' = parent \ {off? ↦ par?} │
│ sex' = sex                │
└───────────────────────────┘
```

Exercises 11.6

1.

$RELATIONSHIP ::= parents \mid grandparents \mid grandchildren \mid descendants \mid siblings \mid aunts$

```
┌─── Relations ──────────────────────────────┐
│ Ξ GenDB                                      │
│ x?: PERSON                                   │
│ rel?: RELATIONSHIP                           │
│ rels! : ℙ PERSON                             │
├──────────────────────────────────────────────┤
│ x? ∈ dom sex                                 │
│ rel? = parents ⇒ rels! = parent({x?})        │
│ rel? = grandparents ⇒ rels! = parent ; parent({x?}) │
│ rel? = grandchildren ⇒ rels! = (parent ; parent)⁻¹({x?}) │
│ rel? = descendants ⇒ rels! = (parent⁻¹)⁺({x?}) │
│ rel? = siblings ⇒ rels! = (parent ; parent⁻¹) \ id PERSON │
│ rel? = aunts ⇒ rels!                          │
│    = {y : PERSON | x?(((parent ; parent) ; parent⁻¹) \ parent) y │
│        ∧ sex y = female}                      │
└──────────────────────────────────────────────┘
```

2.

$\{p : \text{dom } sex \mid p \notin \text{dom } parent \cup \text{ran } parent\}$

3.

$\{p : \text{dom } sex \mid p \notin \text{dom}(parent \, ; parent^{-1}) \setminus \text{id } PERSON)\}$

4.

```
_____ MaxGen _____
Ξ GenDB
p? : PERSON
n : ℕ
──────────────────────────────────────────────
p? ∈ dom sex
p ∈ dom parentⁿ ∧ ∀m : ℕ | m > n • p ∉ dom parentᵐ
```

$p? \in \text{dom } sex$

$p \in \text{dom } parent^n \wedge \forall m : \mathbb{N} \mid m > n \bullet p \notin \text{dom } parent^m$

References

Barden, Rosalind, Stepney, Susan and Cooper, David (1994) *Z in Practice*, Prentice Hall, Hemel Hempstead.

Diller, Antoni (1994) *Z: An introduction to formal methods*, 2nd edition, John Wiley, Chichester.

Directorate of Standardisation, UK Ministry of Defence (1989) Interim defence standard 00-55: Requirements for the procurement of safety critical software in defence equipment.

Hayes, Ian J. (ed.) (1993) *Specification Case Studies*, 2nd edition, Prentice Hall, Hemel Hempstead.

Kelly, John (1997) *The Essence of Logic*, Prentice Hall, Hemel Hempstead.

Spivey, Michael J. (1992) *The Z Notation: A Reference Manual*, 2nd edition, Prentice Hall, Hemel Hempstead.

Stepney, Susan, Barden, Rosalind and Cooper,David (eds) (1992) *Object orientation in Z*, Workshops in Computing, Springer Verlag.

Woodcock, John and Davies, Jim (1996) *Using Z: Specification, Refinement and Proof*, Prentice Hall, Hemel Hempstead.

Glossary

Abbreviation definition
The == sign denotes an abbreviation definition, which is used to introduce a global constant into a specification.

Abstraction
Specifications may be constructed at different levels of abstraction. A high level of abstraction means that the specification concentrates on the essentials and ignores the details of the problem, and a lower level of abstraction means the specification includes more details.

And ($\wedge$)
Binary logic connective. $P \wedge Q$ is true if and only if P and Q are both true.

Axiomatic description
A graphical Z construct for defining a global constant.

Backward composition
The backward composition of relations $S: B \leftrightarrow C$ and $R: A \leftrightarrow B$ is denoted by $S \circ R$ and is the relation of type $A \leftrightarrow C$ such that $S \circ R = R \,; S$, where $R \,; S$ is the **Forward composition** of R and S.

Basic type
Also called a *given set*. A type introduced into a specification by giving a name in square brackets, with an accompanying explanation. No indication is given as to how individual members of the type are represented.

'Before' and 'after' states
To specify an operation on the state of a system, we give predicates defined in terms of the state variables both 'before' and 'after' the operation. The convention is that the names of 'before' variables are undecorated, while the names of 'after' variables are decorated with primes (dashes).

Bijection
A function is a bijection iff it is an **Injection**, a **Surjection** and is **Total**.

Binary relation
A binary relation between sets A and B is any subset of the **Cartesian product** $A \times B$.

Boolean algebra

Propositional logic and set theory are examples of *boolean algebras*. There are five basic laws, or postulates, of boolean algebra from which other laws, or theorems, may be deduced.

Cardinality

The number of elements in a set S is called its *cardinality*, denoted by $\#S$.

Cartesian product

The cartesian product of sets A and B, denoted by $A \times B$, is the set of all ordered pairs such that the first element in each pair is from A and the second element in each pair is from B.

$$A \times B = \{a : A, b : B \bullet a \mapsto b\}$$

Comprehension

A set comprehension is a set-valued expression employing a predicate and an expression which together characterise the members of the set. The form of a set comprehension is {declaration | predicate • expression}.

Concatenation

The concatenation operator $^\frown$ takes two sequences as arguments and returns the sequence formed by 'joining them together'.

Contradiction

A proposition which is false for all possible combinations of the values of its operands.

Declaration

See **Variable**, **Type**.

Deduction

In boolean algebra, the process of proving laws by repeated application of previously derived laws.

Delta convention

For a given schema S, the notation ΔS represents the schema obtained by including S and S' in an otherwise empty schema. For a given state schema S, the inclusion of ΔS in an operation schema indicates that the operation potentially changes the state.

Disjoint

A sequence of sets $\langle A_1, A_2, \ldots, A_n \rangle$ are *pairwise disjoint* if none of the sets intersect with each other. This is tested using the expression disjoint $\langle A_1, A_2, \ldots, A_n \rangle$.

Domain
The domain of a binary relation $R : A \leftrightarrow B$, denoted by dom R, is that subset of A consisting of the first elements from each of the ordered pairs in R, i.e. all the elements which have an arrow emerging from them in the 'picture' of R.

Domain anti-restriction operator
Given a binary relation $R : A \leftrightarrow B$ and a set $S \subseteq A$, R domain anti-restricted to S, denoted by $S \lhd\!\!\!- R$, defines a relation which is the result of removing from R all pairs with first elements that are members of S.

Domain restriction operator
Given a binary relation $R : A \leftrightarrow B$ and a set $S \subseteq A$, R domain restricted to S, denoted by $S \lhd R$, defines a relation which is the result of removing from R all pairs with first elements that are not members of S.

Duality
All of the laws of boolean algebra come in pairs. Given one valid law in, for example, propositional logic, we can derive another one, its *dual*, by replacing all instances of $\wedge$ with $\vee$ and vice versa, and similarly with all instances of *false* and *true*.

Equivalence ($\Leftrightarrow$)
Binary logic connective. $P \Leftrightarrow Q$ may be read as 'P is equivalent to Q' or 'P if and only if Q'.

Existential quantifier
$\exists$ is the symbol for the existential quantifier, used to construct a proposition of the form $\exists \langle name \rangle : \langle type \rangle \mid \langle optional\ constraint \rangle \bullet \langle predicate \rangle$ which is read as 'There exists a $\langle name \rangle$ of type $\langle type \rangle$ for which $\langle optional\ constraint \rangle$ is true, such that $\langle predicate \rangle$ is true.

Extension
We write down a set-valued expression in extension by enumerating the elements between curly brackets, separated by commas.

Filter
The filter operator $\upharpoonright$ takes a sequence and a set of the same type as the sequence's range set, and returns the sequence formed by removing all maplets which do not contain, as their second element, members of the set.

Forward composition
The forward composition of relations $R : A \leftrightarrow B$ and $S : B \leftrightarrow C$, denoted by $R \,\mathbf{;}\, S$, is the relation of type $A \leftrightarrow C$ which may be defined as follows:

$$R \,\mathbf{;}\, S = \{a : A;\ c : C \mid \exists b : B \bullet a \mapsto b \in R \wedge b \mapsto c \in S) \bullet a \mapsto c\}$$

Informally, a maplet $x \mapsto y$ is a member of $R \,\mathbf{;}\, S$ iff you can get from x to y in the picture of R and S by following two consecutive arrows.

Free type
A means of introducing a new type into a specification by enumerating the names of the elements of the type.

Front
A function which returns the sequence formed by removing the last maplet in a non-empty sequence.

Function
A relation $f: A \leftrightarrow B$ is a function iff every element of dom f is mapped to precisely one member of ran f. See **Total function**, **Partial function**.

Function application
For a function $f: A \rightarrow B$, the expression fx where $x \in A$, is read as 'f applied to x', and is the element y of B such that $x \mapsto y \in f$.

Function overriding
The overriding operator, $\oplus$, may be applied to any two functions f and g, of the same type, and the result is another function of the same type. $f \oplus g$ is read as 'f overridden by g', and is a function which behaves the same as f when applied to objects not in the domain of g, and behaves as g otherwise.

Generalised intersection
The generalised intersection of a set of sets S, written as $\bigcap S$, is the set comprising those elements which are members of all the members of S.

Generalised union
The generalised union of a set of sets S, written as $\bigcup S$, is the set of all elements which are members of at least one of the members of S.

Generic constant
A Z construct for defining a constant function, relation or other object in terms of one or more generic formal parameters, which stand for any actual parameter set supplied implicitly or explicitly when the object is used.

Head
A function which returns the first range element in a non-empty sequence.

Homogeneous relation
For a relation $R: A \leftrightarrow B$, if A and B are the same set, the relation is said to be homogeneous.

Identity relation
The identity relation on a set X is id $X = \{x : X \bullet x \mapsto x\}$ that is, the relation which maps every element of X to itself.

Implication ($\Rightarrow$)
Binary logic connective. $P \Rightarrow Q$ is read as 'P implies Q' or 'if P then Q'.

Injection
A function f is an injection (or is one-to-one) iff every value in ran f occurs in precisely one maplet in f. In other words, there are no converging arrows in the picture of f.

Injective sequence
A **Sequence** with no repeated elements. Declared as s : iseq T, where T is a type.

Inputs and outputs
Often required in defining operations. The convention is that an input identifier is terminated by a ? and an output identifier is terminated by a !

Intersection
The intersection of two sets S and T, written as $S \cap T$, is the set consisting of all the members which are in both S and T.

Inverse of a relation
The inverse of a binary relation R, denoted by R^{-1}, is the relation obtained by reversing the order of all the ordered pairs in R; in other words, reversing the direction of all the arrows in the picture of R.

Last
A function which returns the last range element in a non-empty sequence.

Let predicate
A method for naming subexpressions in complex predicates. **let** $n = e \bullet p$ stands for the predicate p, but wherever the name n occurs in p, it represents the value e.

Logical connective
Operators used to create compound propositions by combining other propositions. See **And, Or, Not, Implication** and **Equivalence**.

Maplet
See **Ordered pair**.

Membership
The set membership operator $\in$ is used to test whether an object is a member of a set. The expression $n \in S$ is read as 'n is a member of set S'. Non-membership is tested using $\notin$.

Not ($\neg$)
Unary logic connective. $\neg P$ is true when P is false, and vice versa.

Or ($\vee$)
Binary logic connective. $P \vee Q$ is true when either or both of P and Q are true.

Ordered pair
An ordered pair (a, b) consists of two elements; a is the first element and b is the second element. In Z, ordered pairs are represented by the *maplet* notation $a \mapsto b$.

Partial function
A partial function $f: A \nrightarrow B$ is a function for which elements of the source set A are not necessarily mapped to elements of the target set B. See **Function, Total function**.

Partition
A sequence of sets $\langle A_1, A_2, \ldots, A_n \rangle$ partitions a set S iff the union of all the sets in the sequence is S, and the sets in the sequence are pairwise disjoint; that is, none of the sets intersect with each other. This is written as $\langle A_1, A_2, \ldots, A_n \rangle$ partition S.

Perfect induction
In boolean algebra, the process of proving laws using truth tables – we write down the truth tables for each side of the law, and check that they are identical.

Postcondition
A predicate which defines the effect of an operation by relating the 'before' state and inputs, if any, to the 'after' state and outputs, if any.

Powerset
The powerset of a set S, denoted by $\mathbb{P}S$, is the set of all the subsets of S.

Precondition
A predicate which states what must be true about the 'before' state of a system and the inputs, if any, in order for an operation to successfully take place.

Predicate
An expression containing one or more *free variables* which act as placeholders for values drawn from specified sets. Substituting values for all the free variables in the expression yields a proposition.

Proper subset
For any given sets S, T the expression $S \subset T$ is read as 'S is a proper subset of T', and is a predicate which is true iff every member of S is a member of T and $S \neq T$. See **Subset**.

Proposition
A statement which is either true or false; that is, which has one of the two truth values T or F.

Quantifier
See **Universal quantifier, Existential quantifier**.

Query operation

An operation which does not change the state of a system, but outputs some information about the state.

Range

The range of a binary relation $R : A \leftrightarrow B$, denoted by ran R, is that subset of B consisting of the second elements from each of the ordered pairs in R, i.e. all the elements which have an arrow entering them in the 'picture' of R.

Range anti-restriction operator

Given a binary relation $R : A \leftrightarrow B$, and a set $T \subseteq B$, R range anti-restricted to T, denoted by $R \rhd\!\!\!- T$, defines a relation which is the result of removing from R all pairs with second elements that are members of T.

Range restriction operator

Given a binary relation $R : A \leftrightarrow B$, and a set $T \subseteq B$, R range restricted to T, denoted by $R \rhd T$, defines a relation which is the result of removing from R all pairs with second elements that are not members of T.

Reflexive transitive closure

The reflexive transitive closure of a relation R, denoted by R^*, is the relation obtained by taking the union of all R^n for $n \geqslant 0$. It is equal to $R^+ \cup R^0$, where R^+ is the **Transitive closure** of R and R^0 is the **Identity relation**.

Relational image

Given a binary relation $R : A \leftrightarrow B$ and a set $S \subseteq A$, the relational image of S in R, denoted by $R(S)$, is the set of all those members of ran R which are related to members of S by R.

Rev

A function which returns the sequence formed by reversing the order of the elements in a given sequence.

Schema

A box-like graphical structure used to combine declarations with predicates constraining their values. May be used to describe the state of a system, or operations to modify or interrogate a system state. Schemas may be combined to create new schemas using the various operations of the schema calculus.

Schema composition

The composition of two operation schemas A and B is a schema which specifies the effect of doing operation A followed by operation B. It is written $A \,\fatsemi\, B$.

Schema decoration

Given a schema S, the notation S' stands for S with all of its variables decorated with primes throughout the schema.

Schema definition

$\hat{=}$ is the *schema definition symbol*, which is used to associate a name with a schema expression.

Schema hiding

The schema hiding operator $\setminus$ takes a schema and a list of variables declared in the schema, and hides the variables in the schema by removing them from the schema declarations and existentially quantifying them in the schema predicates. In general, for a schema S, the expression $S \setminus (x, y, z)$ represents S with the declarations of variables x, y and z removed and existentially quantified.

Schema inclusion

All declarations and predicates from a schema S may be included in a schema T by simply placing the name of S in the declaration part of T.

Schema operators

New schemas can be constructed from old ones using propositional operators, decoration, inclusion, the delta and xi conventions, and various other operators.

Schema precondition operator

The schema precondition operator, denoted by pre, is used to calculate the precondition of an operation schema. For an operation schema S, the expression pre S is the precondition schema of S, which is S with all 'after' state variables and output variables hidden.

Schema renaming

Schema variables may be renamed to produce a new schema, by writing the necessary changes in square brackets after the schema name. In general, for a schema S, the expression $S\,[x\,/\,a,\,y\,/\,b,\,z\,/\,c]$ represents S with all instances of the name a replaced by x, b by y and c by z.

Sequence

A sequence s is a function, the domain of which is a prefix subset of $\mathbb{N}_1$, the natural numbers excluding zero. In other words, dom $s = 1 .. \#s$. Declared as $s : \text{seq } T$, where T is a type.

Set

A collection of distinct objects called *elements* or *members*. See **Type**, **Extension**, **Comprehension**.

Set difference

The difference of two sets S and T, written as $S \setminus T$, is the set consisting of all the members of S which are not in T.

Set equality

Two sets are equal iff they contain exactly the same members.

Source set
For a binary relation $R: A \leftrightarrow B$, A is called the source set.

Squash
The *squash* function takes any function f such that $\operatorname{dom} f \subseteq \mathbb{N}_1$ and returns the sequence formed by modifying the domain of f, maintaining the original order which it defines.

State invariant
A predicate defining the invariant properties of the state of a system, i.e. properties which must not change as the system moves from state to state.

Subset
For any given sets S, T the expression $S \subseteq T$ is read as 'S is a subset of T', and is a predicate which is true iff every member of S is a member of T.

Surjection
The function $f: A \twoheadrightarrow B$ is a surjection (*onto* its target) iff every value in B is mapped to by the function, i.e. $\operatorname{ran} f = B$.

Tail
A function which returns the sequence formed by removing the first maplet in a non-empty sequence and, if necessary, modifying the domain of the result to make it a sequence, maintaining the original order.

Target set
For a binary relation $R: A \leftrightarrow B$, B is called the target set.

Tautology
A proposition which is true for all possible combinations of the values of its operands.

Total function
A total function $f: A \to B$ is a partial function for which every element of the source set A is mapped to an element of the target set B; that is $\operatorname{dom} f = A$. See **Function, Partial function**.

Total operation
An operation which specifies the action to be taken for all possible values of the state variables and inputs.

Transitive closure
The transitive closure of a relation R, denoted by R^+, is the relation obtained by taking the union of all R^n for $n > 0$.

Truth table
A means of writing down the truth value of a logic expression for each combination of the truth values of its operand propositions.

Type

A maximal set. Every **Variable** and expression must be associated with a type from which its value(s) must be drawn. See also **Basic type**, **Free type**.

Union

The union of two sets S and T, written as $S \cup T$, is the set consisting of all the members from S and T.

Universal quantifier

$\forall$ is the symbol for the universal quantifier, used to construct a proposition of the form $\forall \langle \text{name} \rangle : \langle \text{type} \rangle \mid \langle \text{optional constraint} \rangle \bullet \langle \text{predicate} \rangle$, which is read as 'for all $\langle \text{name} \rangle$ of type $\langle \text{type} \rangle$ such that $\langle \text{optional constraint} \rangle$ is true, $\langle \text{predicate} \rangle$ is true'.

Variable

A name which stands for a value. Introduced into a specification by writing a *declaration* associating the name with a **Type** from which its values must be drawn.

Xi convention

For a given state schema S, the notation ΞS represents the schema obtained by including ΔS in an otherwise empty schema together with, for every variable x declared in S, the predicate $x = x'$. Including ΞS in an operation schema asserts that S is not changed by the operation.

Index